Kimono
Vanishing Tradition

Japanese Textiles of the 20th Century

Cheryl Imperatore
&
Paul MacLardy

Schiffer Publishing Ltd

4880 Lower Valley Road, Atglen, PA 19310 USA

Title Page: Photo by L. A. Clever

Library of Congress Cataloging-in-Publication Data

Imperatore, Cheryl.
Kimono vanishing tradition: Japanese textiles of the 20th century / Cheryl Imperatore
and Paul MacLardy.
p. cm.
ISBN 0-7643-1228-6 (hardcover)
1. Kimonos--History. 2. Textile fabrics--Japan--History--20th century. 3. Textile design--Japan--
History--20th century. I. MacLardy, Paul. II. Title.
GT1560 I46 2000
391'.00952--dc21
00-011041

Designed by Bonnie M. Hensley
Cover designed by Bruce M. Waters
Type set in Brush 455 BT/Benguiat Bk BT

ISBN: 0-7643-1228-6
Printed in China
1 2 3 4

Published by Schiffer Publishing Ltd.
4880 Lower Valley Road
Atglen, PA 19310
Phone: (610) 593-1777; Fax: (610) 593-2002
E-mail: Schifferbk@aol.com
Please visit our web site catalog at **www.schifferbooks.com**

In Europe, Schiffer books are distributed by Bushwood Books
6 Marksbury Avenue Kew Gardens
Surrey TW9 4JF England
Phone: 44 (0) 20-8392-8585; Fax: 44 (0) 20-8392-9876
E-mail: Bushwd@aol.com
Free postage in the UK. Europe: air mail at cost.

This book may be purchased from the publisher. Include $3.95 for shipping.
Please try your bookstore first.
We are always looking for people to write books on new and related subjects. If you have an idea for a book please contact us
at the Atglen, PA address.

You may write for a free catalog.

Dedication

To the past...
To the memories of Eugene and Margaret Virginia Imperatore
To the Future...
To Bryn

Acknowledgements

We thank Ann Marie Moeller for her special knowledge, enthusiasm and assistance. Other Arise employees who contributed are Teena Turner and Julie Cimino. It is from Shizumi Shigeto Manale's recollections that many of the kimono in this book were assigned dates. The textile artists represented were contacted through Arise, Inc. or by personal association with the authors.

Photo by Ken Wyner.

Author's Preface

My first Japanese textile absorbed my attention because of its many charms - it was a deep plum colored chevron weave heavy silk called *chirimen*, with a surface of woven satin that was stenciled with a colorful flower, lined with a tri-colored tie dyed light silk I've come to know as *shibori*, and having two handwoven closures of a softly colored gold cord. It was 1983, and I was a prowler of thrift shops for funky vintage; I couldn't imagine someone having so wonderful a garment and abandoning it. It smoothed over my shoulders and fell to just above my knee. I was smitten.

Boxes of vintage Japanese goods had been hauled into a cafe where I was working by a couple who led tours to Japan to promote the nuclear freeze movement. They financed their good works by selling kimono. I was cooking at the cafe, and also volunteering my advertising and publicity skills through my business Arise. Paul MacLardy was also on this committee. We held a successful fund raiser by displaying and selling the kimono off the walls of the restaurant.

I fell in love with the fabrics and techniques of Japanese traditional garments and began working with this couple to learn more. I collected more examples of the work.

In 1986, the couple decided to attend graduate school out of the area. Instead of Arise Advertising, I became, with my now partner, Paul MacLardy, Arise - Window to the East, and plunged into retail. I remember a trip I made to the Small Business Association for information on setting up and making this a real business. It provoked incredulity on the part of the advisors. "You want to sell *schmatas*?" they asked, an old Yiddish term for rags. I'm sure they thought I was a *meschuggnah shicksa* - crazy non-Jewish woman.

Paul and I went to Japan on a buying trip and at first sold our goods at street markets and what we called "New Age Tupperware™ parties," as we would arrange fund-raisers for different political and social issues we felt strongly about, and haul boxes of kimono for people to try on and buy. Eventually we opened a store in the Takoma section of Washington, D. C. Paul still operates this business, which has grown to encompass many other areas. I focus on mail order and personal buying for customers.

I am by no means a scholar on Japanese textiles, but possess a certain knowledge gained from handling thousands of examples in recent years and researching to find out more about their intriguing qualities. I found many interesting and informative sites on the World Wide Web that more completely filled in the information that was gathered through my own experience. In May of 1997, *Threads* magazine published my article on working with these fabrics, and I have lectured at the Textile Museum and at The World Bank, both in Washington, D. C.

Over the years I have absorbed some of the details of the way of Japanese dressing which I enjoy passing along. I hope this work encourages you to explore these fascinating and quickly disappearing remnants of a once-elaborate cultural tradition.

Cheryl Imperatore

I remember my first trip to Japan. I took the *shinkensan* (bullet train) to central Japan where I was met by the kimono dealer. We spent the next three days across from each other with stacks of kimono folded in half long-wise. With each of us holding one end, I inspected one side, we turned it, I inspected the other side, and then we opened it to inspect the middle. I would say either "*ire nai*" (no) or "*oh na gai shi mas*" (I want)...all this in the space of thirty seconds.

How absorbing it was to personally inspect thousands of kimono and see the endless range of techniques and patterns and the personal touches added by the original owners. In those days it was just Cheryl and me running our business.

Fifteen years later, Arise has grown to encompass textiles and antiques from all over Asia with a large staff, but I still personally inspect each kimono that comes into Arise and price them. Having seen literally hundreds of thousands of kimono, I can safely say I am still amazed by the variations I see.

It is only fitting that, as this book nears completion, I have just returned from a buying trip to Japan where I spent my last day at a textiles auction. There I was, with all these Japanes dealers, on my knees, inspecting the textiles up for auction, holding them up to the light and occasionally saying, "*oh na gai she mas*"...

A textile's condition and the uniqueness of the item always affect their value. Prices of new kimono of excellent quality can be over $10,000, and with the obi and other accessories it can be over $15,000. An uchikake (wedding kimono) new is over $25,000. Vintage kimono are not expensive at this point, but as they disappear prices are rising quickly, particularly for kimono utilizing rare techniques that are disappearing.

Paul MacLardy

Contents

Background

There are no *kimonos* in this book; the plural of kimono is kimono. It is pronounced with a short first syllable (kee-*moh*-no). It means simply "thing to wear." It is only one part of a complex costume that is worn less often by Japanese people. Some pronunciation guides in the text are intended for interested readers; however, it is not necessary to know how to pronounce Japanese words to appreciate and collect Japanese textiles. In reading aloud a Japanese word, be advised every syllable is pronounced, and most syllables are two to three letters in length.

The woman standing at the fence says goodbye to her visitor. Both are wearing *meisen fudangi, ikat* visiting kimono. Early 20th century photo.

The art of dressing— as known to the Japanese in the twentieth century and previously— will be all but gone in the twenty-first century. From a design and embellishment standpoint, the images exhibited by older garments has changed with fashion over time. Techniques and details of decorative techniques still being done in the twentieth century are listed and approximate dates are given to most items in the book. Hand crafting these clothes was a project with many phases, and many hands and minds were involved in the process: weaving, dyeing, decorating, and sewing. The person who wore the garment gave it their personal style and distinction through the selection of *obi, getta,* fans, and *inro.*

The prosperity of the Japanese people from about 1960 to the mid-1990s has made it possible for Japanese women today to own from a few to many kimono. This book covers the styles available to them, from the simple everyday kimono(*fudangi*) to the visiting kimono(*homongi*) and formal kimono(*tomesode*). To successfully collect Japanese vintage textiles, you must see beyond the garment in front of you into its past and imagine who wore it and how it was worn before you decide to proceed with a collection. Your eye should guide you in any collecting venture, and with textiles the hand and heart are involved as well.

Oftentimes with vintage textiles, and kimono in particular, the parts are greater than the whole. Although we can purchase silk yardage in fine fabric stores today, getting and taking apart a Japanese garment can be more satisfying. The standard length of material used for a kimono garment is a *tan*, about 12 yards. The width of Japanese material is between 14 and 15 inches.

Photo, see page 22.

A lining fabric, probably from a haori, that touts a record label, probably from the late Taisho period.

Fabric length with strong graphic design of paulownia, a favored image.

Bales with wires or twine actually securing kimono like hay were popular for a time, but the difficulty in restoring the garment to its original shape after such compaction is extremely arduous. You may be left only with the wonderful silk, and there is a broad range of it.

The variety of kimono patterns and prints, from stripes to jacquard, is a nostalgic trip through the century. Students of fashion and culture can put a date on the style of material used. Contemporary wearable artists and surface designers sometimes utilize the kimono design as is, by assembling the simple three-rectangle shape into a new expression of their art, or by taking pieces of the fabric and creating something entirely new: cutting and resewing, over dyeing, studying the original fabrics and making it their own by re-interpreting it.

Interior designers also utilize Japanese textiles to great advantage in oriental decor. Obi become pillows, wall hangings or table runners; kimono are made into luxurious bedspreads.

The chances of finding that perfect condition, all-over embroidered kimono in colors to match your decorating scheme are slender, but possible. Make use of resources in many areas. Check thrift stores, estate sales, boutiques, mail order, and these days the internet to get knowledge of what is available.

Yardage of Japanese design but in a double width, perhaps made when machinery began producing material and traditional looms became a thing of the past.

The Vintage Vantage Point

The age-old art and craft of hand weaving, dyeing, sewing and embellishing clothing is quickly disappearing from most traditional cultures. The Japanese have taken dressing very seriously, and until the early to mid-twentieth century most of its people wore kimono most of the time. People were supportive of the kimono industry and artisans, and many were able to afford extensive kimono wardrobes for their families. In the 1900s a well-to-do woman may have had three hudred personal kimono —almost a different one for every day of the year— so they were an expression, albeit understated, of personal style. Until the middle part of the twentieth century, the Japanese people engaged in a hierarchy of clothing and dressing that was vastly more complex than in many other cultures of this time.

During the twentieth century, cultures all over the world have met and merged, and this is most reflected in what people wear. We have a recognized world uniform of suits, dresses, pants and shirts that more-or-less look alike. Mass production of clothing by machines has made this possible. The traditional form of dress is disappearing as most of Japan's population adheres to western dress. Before the 1940s, everyone wore them.

Japanese people are fastidious about the condition and appearance of their kimono. If stains or spots cannot be removed, the kimono is given away. Think of how these women would carefully move among the sprays of the waterfall at Tamadare. If the crepe of their kimono puckered or delicate hand painting ran, it might have turned up in a temple sale.

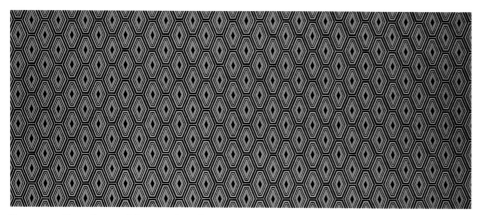

Screen pattern is used for men's yukata. Men's patterns are usually small and geometric.

Two lengths of lightweight wool or rayon yardage, pre-1920, with rabbits. In the middle is a woman's ikat jacket, made of oshima silk, lined in another interesting fabric.

From the lining of a man's haori, this design is probably silk-screened.

A man's nagajuban has this colorful design of a samurai helmet.

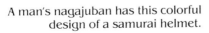

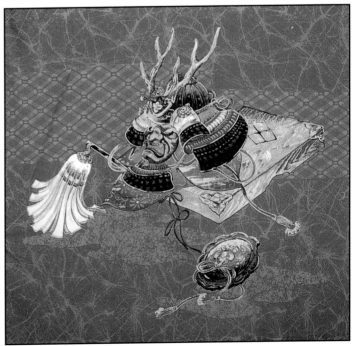

Today, the people of Japan have almost completely shed the last layer of a centuries-old tradition of a highly valued, highly artistic form of dress generally classified as the kimono. Kimono are usually seen only at weddings or other ceremonial or religious occasions. They are a vanishing breed of hand sewn, and many times hand decorated, silk and cotton clothing.

Preserving and protecting a work of fine textile craftsmanship therefore is left to a very few. Japan promotes and protects its weavers, dyers and sewers of kimono as National Treasures, and funds apprenticeships for people willing to learn the crafts; but few sign on.

It is likely that many Japanese women born in the twenty-first century will never own a kimono. Kimono are worn only very occasionally, and are not easily adapted to contemporary life. If a young woman wanted to wear a kimono in Japan today, she would most likely go to a school to learn about it, whereas in the past, she would have learned by observing her mother, aunts and grandmother. This book showcases these types of kimono.

Ikat detail of kimono, showing mending where it has been worn through.

Screens cut from persimmon tree bark are used to create the repeat pattern on yukata fabric.

Textile Techniques

Japanese textiles are categorized by 1) the type of weave, 2) whether its surface is finished before or after it is dyed, and 3) what kind of embellishment or surface design is added after dyeing.

1. Types of Weaves

Woven designs

Weaving is an intensive process. It can take twenty-five days or more to weave twelve yards of material.

Ikat is a process whereby either or both the weft and the warp are bound and dyed previous to being woven, and the pattern emerges on the loom. The Japanese have interpreted this in many ways: *kasuri*, splashed cloth is often seen in farmer's cotton clothing of indigo and white. *Meisen* (may-sen) was popular in the early twentieth century as women began entering the work force and it was sturdy and easier to clean. When fine silk is spun, it is pulled and reeled from cocoons, and the leftover product is silk floss which has a slub, or irregularity. *Oshima* and *tsumugi* pongee are special types of ikat the the Japanese highly prize that are made from floss. *Jofu* is a type of ramie, a linen like material produced from stiff fibers for summer wear. It is also often an ikat.

Blue rinzu silk of waves and pine trees, with supplementary warp lacquered threads of silver and red.

Jun-hitoe are single layered kimono, often woven by a method called *sha*, which though appearing sheer, can have two designs or contrasting warp and weft threads which give it a changing appearance. *Ro* silk resembles horizontal rows of silk, and has an airy, light feel though is often used for black kimono or haori. The technique of weqving a figured silk resembling jacquard came from the Chinese. It is referred to here as *rinzo*.

The Japanese especially revere the weavers of obi, as they feel it expresses "the good taste and the opulence of their hearts... (to) refinement" (Kenichi Kawakatsu, "Kimono,"Japan Travel Bureau,1936, p.36).

Gauzy gray silk with silvery dragon-flies flitting through the fibers, through the magic of weaving.

A design element of a silver section of a peacock feather from an unlined summer kimono.

From an Edo period wedding kimono, two shades of lacquered threads are woven on top of blue figured silk.

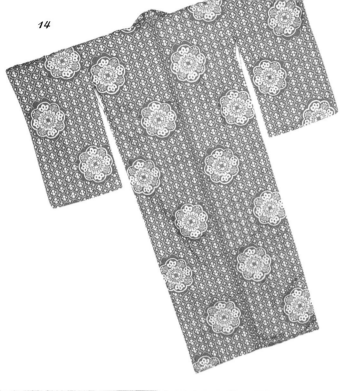

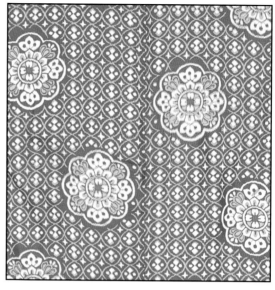

Late 1950s to early 1960s, possibly polyester. Medallion, flower design with all over interlocking circles. $60-90

A beautiful ikat design on a kimono that, at a distance, gives the appearance of a watercolor.

Two western influenced meisen ikat haori. Linings are bold print fabric. Mid-Taisho. $150-200 each

A machine woven element from a kimono sleeve.

Two kimono sections; the gray one was probably woven by hand and the light one by machine.

A complicated woven design on a kimono from the 1950s.

2. *Surface Finished Before or After Dyeing*

Tie Dyed Cloth

Shibori - a resist and dye process that utilizes a variety of methods, such as clamping, wrapping, binding, stitching, or folding, to achieve a dimensional shaped cloth. The texture of the cloth is often part of its appearance, however, it is also used flat to show the design dyed in.

Tiny areas of cloth are tightly stitched and thread is wound to prevent dye from penetrating. When this is done over the entire surface of the material, it is called *kanoko*, of which there are at least five types. Cloth can also be sewn tightly into patterns that will resemble woodgrain or waves, or geometric forms when the threads are snipped after the dyeing process is finished.

Wrapping cloth around pole and securing it is called *arashi* or storm by the Japanese. When cloth is capped, an impenetrable material is used, such as oiled paper or plastic to permit the dye to color outside the area. This is called *chuboshi* or *oboshi*. (Yoshiko Wada, Mark Kellogg Rice, and Jane Barton, *Shibori: The Inventive Art of Japanese Shaped Resist Dyeing*, New York: Kodansha International/USA Ltd., 1983.)

Women's nagajuban dyed diagonal in colors that would usually be considered a men's. Shibori dots are made like stylized letters. Has been taken up at waist and in at shoulders. Lined in white cotton, with string resembling a shoelace sewn in the middle of the back. *Good Goods Collection.* $150-200

This photo shows the lining of a simple black haori. The vivid colors and complex shibori design make this one that easily could be worn inside out.

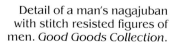

Detail of a man's nagajuban with stitch resisted figures of men. *Good Goods Collection.*

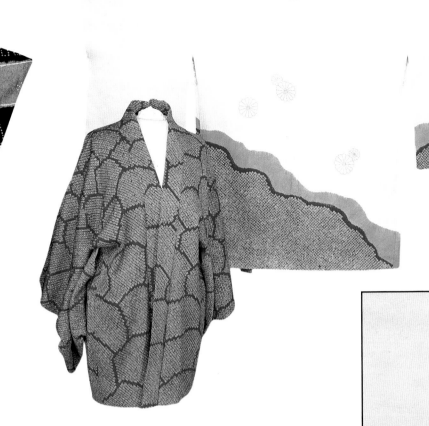

Shibori can be done in many ways. Here two examples of haori in white and red, with all over design resembling tortoise shell and one on pole showing back design resembling water flowing.

A detail from a woman's nagajuban showing a koi and bubbles created using shibori, with a lacquered thread detail of a water eddy.

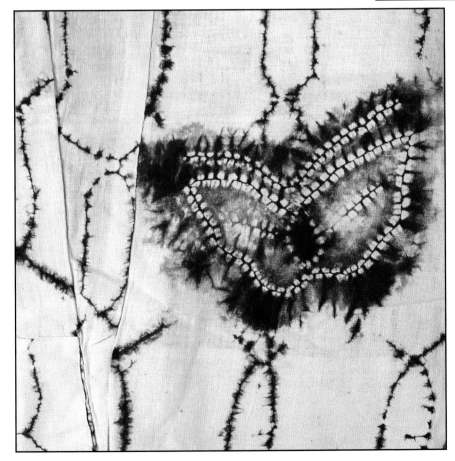

A butterfly captured on a white cotton yukata, probably from early twentieth century.

Dyeing with stencils

Katazome - a stenciled design, most often produced in Japanese textiles by using rice paste resist, although sometimes wax is used, much like batiked cloth. Aizome is indigo cloth that has be dyed using this method.

Bingata cloth from Okinawa is distinctive in its use of primary colored dyes.

Painting on Silk

Yuzen - the art of painting on silk within a resisted area was introduced by a man, Miyazaki Yuzensai from Kyoto, during the Genroku period (1688-1704). He used a mixture of rice paste, soybeans and salt that was stored in a container like a pastry bag. The tip of the bag was used to make a design that was more free than the traditional stencils.

Sumi e painting is done free hand using indelible inks and a bamboo brush. The inks are compressed into brick form. Tiny water pots add drops until the right consistency or color is achieved, then the master commits the brush to the cloth to swiftly complete the design. It is one thing to do this on paper; on silk the whole twelve yards necessary for the kimono are vulnerable.

From the 1980s, this indigo dyed kimono is printed on heavy chirimen silk.

By displaying this kimono flat on the ground, the artist's completeness of vision is seen, as well as how seamless is the sewer's integration of the parts into the whole. Mid-Showa period. Yuzen painting. $250-350

A detail from the bottom of a sleeve shows the delicacy of late Showa period yuzen painting on a rinzu silk background of lavender.

Unusual lining of a man's haori has all-over embroidery with a background of *sumi-e* painting.

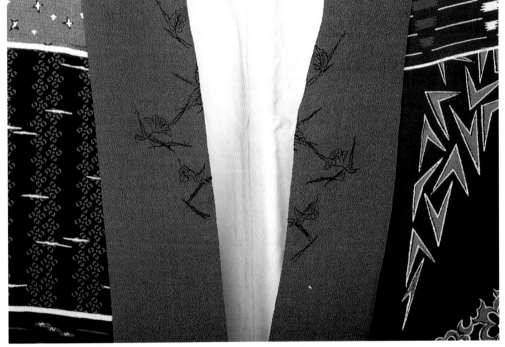

3. Surface Design Added After Dyeing

Embroidery

Nui - embroidery is sometimes delicately added to the petals of flowers, or thin gold threads are floated across a design. The word for satin stitch is *hira-nui*. Couching is called *shusu* , and is a technique whereby thread is wrapped with gold or silver foil, and laid down on the material to be stitched into intricate patterns. This is called *koma-nui* when it is lacquered thread work.

A kimono that has various methods of pink shibori on a white background with white and blue embroidered flowers and couched threads of silver and gold detailing. Stained. About $220; if perfect, about $2000

This collar of a nagajuban, an undergarment, has delicate embroidery that would probably not be visible when worn.

This mon on a man's kimono is stitched with heavy thread, possibly dating it to the early 20th century.

From a chuburisode, this flower is couched with gold threads.

Care and Storage

Normal Care

In earlier times, a kimono of good silk that had faded would be taken apart and re-dyed. Good kimono are never dry cleaned. If you are doing the cleaning yourself, take the garment out of storage periodically and check for insect infestation. It could be cleaned gently by shaking off dust and vacumning all the parts with gentle suction through a piece of screening. Then it can be refolded and put away.

On silk items, a basting thread is sometimes found at the edge of the sleeves. It means either it is *hampa mono*, something made but never sold, or worn then washed and resewn, but never reworn. There is a ritual connected with the snipping (removing) of this basting thread, and it is only done on auspicious days according to the Japanese calender. Days numbered with a 4 or a 9 are bad days to remove the thread. A *ki chi* day is a good one and a *dai ki chi* day is not such a good one. This ritual may be a tradition adapted from China.

In the 1970s and 1980s, a thicker silk was produced that holds its shape and doesn't show signs of wear if it is carefully cleaned and put away.

If the garment is something you love but it has stains you can't abide, take it apart and make it into something else. See chapter 14 on wearable art for some ideas.

An undergarment, nagajuban, that is folded in a traditional Japanese manner.

A new born baby's padded kimono that is unworn but old, possibly from the 1930s. The label is from the Momotaro, which means "peach boy," company. All new garments are stitched closed, and when the stitches are to be snipped, it must be done on an auspicious day, according to Japanese calendars.

Storage

To properly store a kimono, it is wrapped in protective rice paper called *tatoushi*, and laid flat in a drawer. Ideally this would be a *kiri tansu*, a chest made of lightweight wood that repels moisture and is made specifically for kimono. A kimono should not be hung on a hanger or sealed in plastic.

A kimono shape is three rectangles, so you may do a simple folding job to put it away. Make sure your hands are free of soil or oils. Grasp the edges of both sleeves in your right hand, and the point of the collar in your left. The kimono will be open on the left side. Bring the neck towards your body and hold it with your left hand. Use the right hand to fold sleeves over the body. Use your left hand to hold the kimono as you fold it in half, and half again.

The middle section of the tansu holds the kimono wrapped in paper.

A traditional Japanese three-part chest, called a tansu, used to store kimono.

A furisode made in 1998. Shizumi Shigeto Manale stores her kimono in the traditional manner - wrapped in rice paper. The window on the top permits viewing the color and pattern without opening it up. Heisei period.

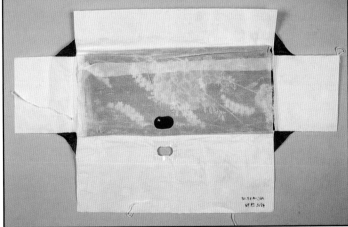

The first layer is untied, revealing an inner, lighter weight rice paper that is also tied.

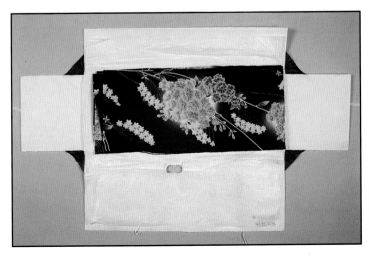

The kimono is stored folded along vertical lines to avoid horizontal wrinkles. To prevent stress on the silk, kimono should never be hung on a hanger.

Display

To display kimono or obi, it is suggested that you do not hang it in direct sunlight. Display it for only a limited amount of time, if you wish to preserve it. Using a smooth bamboo pole, insert along the top of the sleeves, being careful not to snag the kimono. Support the ends and middle if necessary to make a quick and easy wall hanging. Cords and decorative ties for hanging can also be created. Pieces should be examined frequently for signs of insect infestation, as bugs love natural fibers. Locate a professional textile conservator and have a piece framed if you wish to have it permanently protected.

Textile Sources in Japan

Many examples of textiles that are centuries old have been preserved in two particular Japanese temples, one in Nara at the Todai-ji, and one outside Nara at the Horyu-ji. The Tokyo National Museum currently houses many items from these valuable collections that tell us much about Japanese history and culture through the ages. The Kyoto Kimono Society is also a major source of information about old and recent kimono artists.

A delightful collection of fabrics and furniture. On the kimono rack: June Colburn designed wall quilt "Keiko," which uses vintage fabric. On the opposite side, pieces of fabric and a roll of material from the 1920s. The blue and white material on the floor is a "tan" of about 12 yards, enough to make a yukata robe. Next to it are old silk zabuton floor pillows from a Shinto temple. The box on the tansu chest is used for sewing, with needle storage at the top. The rolls of material next to it are for the making of obi. Buckram would be used to give stiffness to hold the obi bow arrangement. Tansu chests usually are two or three pieces that can be stacked and are valued from $2500 and up. Kimono racks in good condition are rare, and do not hold or display a kimono as you would expect - fully open, but draped or folded as a kind of screen. They range in value from $100 to $500, depending on condition. *Furniture from Arise.*

1. History

As in many other Asian cultures, textiles have been utilized extensively in the religious, social and political life of the Japanese people. It is documented that offerings of cloth from China to Japan, and vice versa, were made beginning in the sixth century during the Nara Period (645-794AD) when Nara was the capital city of Japan.

The Heian Period 794-1185

By the Heian Period, Kyoto had become the new capital and Japan severed contact with China. The Japanese court assumed importance as the seat of cultural life, and the custom of elaborate layers of subtly colored robes was popular with the women. *Jun-hitoe*, twelve unlined robes, were frequently worn, with the sleeve edges and collars showing the shadings of each robe.

The Tale of Genji, considered to be the first novel in Japanese, was written by an aristocratic Japanese woman, Murasaki Shikibu, in the eleventh century. She writes descriptively of of the clothing worn by groups of women going on outings, as well as of the fine textiles found in temples. The word *kosode* means small sleeve, and its shape is the forerunner of today's kimono. Persons of the royal court are described competing in the tastefulness of layering their sleeve ends, having them peek out to display a range of silky shades. Sometimes, up to sixteen layers would be worn. Screens and scrolls created during that time showcase the variety of patterns and techniques used in creating these distinctive costumes.

Emperor and Empress dolls from Girl's Day Set, arrayed in front of a gold screen. The dolls wear the costumes of the Heian period, (792-11492 A.D.) These sets are displayed on March 3rd, with the royal couple at the top, and dolls representing the court arrayed on a stepped platform below them. There are 14 dolls plus accessories to a set. Full sets are rare, but individual pieces can be very interesting and beautiful. Mid Showa period. $450-550 pair

The Kamakura period 1185-1333

Characterized by the rising influence of the military class and warriors, people of the Kamakura period had no patience or need for elaborate costumes. Practicality prevailed and opulence, for the most part, was out of fashion. It was during this period that the *kosode*, literally meaning 'small sleeve,' was reintroduced and this form of apparel is closely related to the shape and appearance of the kimono.

The Muromachi and Momoyama periods 1392 - 1600

The 1300 to the 1600s were periods of intense struggles among the military, political and religious factions who fought to assert their control over the islands of Japan. Eventually, the *shogunate*, the military, became the dominant power in Japan.

The Edo period 1603 to 1868

In 1615, military leader Tokugawa Ieyasu moved the capital of the country from Kyoto, where the emperor and his court resided, to Edo, the present day Tokyo. Tokyo remains as a power center for the country.

Japanese leaders apportioned lands to the *daimyo*, who had been leaders of the *samurai* warriors. The creed of Confucianism was adopted by the Tokugawa leaders, and hierarchy became a guiding principle. Ranks of citizens ranged from lowly merchant up to artisan, farmer, and samurai. The regional samurai were required to spend alternate years in residence at the castle in Edo, to insure their loyalty. Their travels became a basis for developing prosperity, since entourages had to be equipped with food, lodging and other supplies along the way.

During the Edo period, people began to define their status by what they wore. Contests to select the most beautiful kimono were a common occurrence, and sometimes the simplest designs won the competition, because of the understated elegance they portrayed. However, during the 17th century sumptuary laws were enacted to limit the mixing of the ranks of people by restricting the opulence of their clothing. But often the rules were ignored or ways around the proclamations were found. For instance, if a certain color was banned from wearing by commoners, another name for a slightly different shade was made, and it quickly became in demand. As a result, prices were very high but some of the greatest artistic accomplishments were made at this time. (Dale Carolyn Gluckman, *When Art Became Fashion*, New York: Weatherhill, 1992, p. 30.)

After 1853, when United States Naval Commander Perry sailed with his fleet into Tokyo harbor with an international ultimatum, the gradual changes taking place in traditional lifestyles in Japan accelerated. His visit marked the beginning of Japan's commercial opening to the Western world. Although Japanese people continued to wear kimono for another hundred years, the beginning of the end of this practice was near.

The Meiji period 1868-1912

The Sino-Japanese War of 1894-95 united the Japanese people in the defense of their country. Women began working outside their homes and required different clothing to accommodate their various obligations. More than most peoples of the world, the Japanese have rituals ingrained in their culture and they appear even in the fabric of their clothing. Meisen silk, an ikat weave, became more popular at the turn of the century, but it was regarded as lower quality than yuzen and embroidered kimono.

The Japanese people developed techniques to compete with the machine-woven and machine-printed cloth available from the West. For example, historically, the village of Arimatsu was known for its shibori (tie dyed cloth) work and it was along the Tokaido Road, so many traveling people passed through it on their way to Edo. In the mid-1800s, the village went into decline because it was not served by the railroad, and people were buying their shibori from other parts of the country.

The Taisho period 1912-1926

During the Taisho period, Tokyo suffered a devastating cultural loss when an earthquake leveled many wooden, bamboo, and paper constructed homes in 1923. Many of the old kimono were lost at that time. As the city and surrounding area was rebuilt, kimono production surged, since "off the shelf" clothing was not available.

The Showa period 1926-1989

The Japanese government curtailed silk production during the late 1920s by taxing it to support their military buildup. Designs then were less complex and material was conserved to permit women to have the appearance of being in fashion, while actually cutting back their use of cloth.

During the first half of the twentieth century, a well-to-do Japanese woman could have had an extensive kimono wardrobe, complete with obi and other acoutrements. A geisha or entertainer may have had as many as three hundred kimono in her wardrobe; items were commissioned to suit their particular needs. People of more modest means had a selection of everyday and visiting kimono made with serviceable silk, and would perhaps rent kimono for ceremonial or wedding occasions.

After World War II, as Japan's economy gradually recovered, kimono became even more affordable and were produced in greater quantities. Style and fashion ideas from Europe and America affected kimono designs and motif interpretations, but their shape and construction remained the same. Colors of kimono and obi changed with the seasons and with the age and status of the wearer. If part of the outfit became worn or soiled, it was sold to a second-hand clothing dealer or donated to a temple. The dealer may then have changed the linings to cotton instead of silk.

Nagagi kimono detail of *bi jin ga* meaning a picture of beautiful women romanticized in the floating world, glimpsed through small sections of screens. Muted colors but very striking design. Printed pattern. Lined entirely in white, with accents at hem and sleeves of flowing sage green, called bokashi. Delightful. $400-$500

This piece has a label in the neck that reads in English "Made in Japan," but the shape is very much like Chinese dress and not Japanese at all. Elaborate hand embroidery and couched threads on rinzu silk of waves. Probably made for sale to tourists who were unfamiliar with the intricacies of the actual kimono, or for a Chinese person living in Japan. Early twentieth century.

Back view. Colors and condition are excellent. *Good Goods Collection.*

The Heisei period 1989 to present

Today, a typical Japanese woman may own only one kimono. This usually is a *furisode*, worn for the coming-of-age ceremony at her nineteenth birthday. For weddings, complete apparel for the entire participating members is usually rented.

Shizumi Shigeto Manale is now living in the United States, but she grew up in Osaka, Japan, where she remembers her mother and grandmother almost always wearing kimono. Because Shizumi is involved with the performance of traditional Japanese dance, she has knowledge of the styles and patterns of twentieth century kimono. Her family members were educators, and have lived outside the city of Hiroshima for over 200 years. It is from her recollections that many of the kimono in this book were assigned dates.

Shizumi's great aunt was the daughter of a geisha who had many well placed acquaintances. This aunt introduced Shizumi to Shigayama Sensaku, the great classical theater master of Kyogen, and a National Living Treasure. Fancy kimono, such as was sold in Kyoto or Tokyo, would not have been appropriate in their town near Hiroshima and, in the early part of the twentieth century, the average girls there each had maybe two or three kimono that were carefully maintained. Material was hand spun and woven because they would not often go to the cities to buy material. The great aunt, however, may have had fifty to a hundred kimono, because her father was a doctor. After he went to England, his daughters became among the first Japanese girls to wear Western clothes in the 1920s.

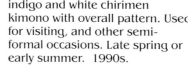

Shizumi's mother instilled in her the aesthetic of the kimono. She recently received a National Culture Merit Award for folk music.

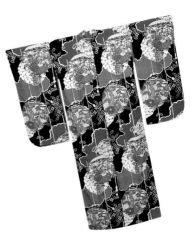

indigo and white chirimen kimono with overall pattern. Used for visiting, and other semi-formal occasions. Late spring or early summer. 1990s.

Zori footwear to match kimono.

A kimono and matching obi, designed in 1999 by Japanese artist. The suggestion of flight is shown by the sweep of a wingtip, in fanciful colors of deep plum and silver. Oburisode sleeves. Newly purchased in Japan, this set would cost between $5000 and 8,000.

Shizumi in costume as a geisha. She performs and lectures to educate groups about disappearing Japanese cultural traditions and the ways of wearing kimono. She wears a *tomesode*. *Photo courtesy of Shizumi Shigeto Manale.*

Opposite page
Right; top to bottom:
A kimono that belonged to Shizumi Shigeto Manale's grandmother, from 1910. Rinzu silk with yuzen design of a drum and flowers.

This kimono belonged to Shizumi's mother. Her mother's name, Midori means green. It was made for her by her grandmother in the late 1940s. After World War II, silk was hard to come by, and the grandmother grew the cocoons and wove the silk. Possibly someone else designed and dyed the material. Finally, she lovingly sewed it for her daughter's wedding chest. It is a family treasure.

A going out kimono belonging to Shizumi Shigeto Manale, that was her mother's originally, from the late 1930s or early 1940s. It was her best kimono at the time. They lived in a rural area, and this was purchased in Kyoto.

A ro kimono with all over design of flowering water and flowers. Made in the style of Okinawan artists, this piece is from the late 1960s. It was worn for a formal occasion, such as attending the springtime wedding of a relative. Collection of Shizumi.

2. Yukata-Cotton Robes

The word yukata (you-kah-tah) is the generally accepted term for the ankle length cotton robe with lines that mimic the silk kimono. Designs for women's yukata have mostly floral and nature derived motifs, and the men's yukata usually have geometric motifs. Indigo and white were the traditional colors used, however personal preference and wider availability of styles now determines this choice. Yukata are actually worn in Japan more than kimono, as they are more comfortable, especially in the summertime. *Yukata-bira* is a term for putting on the robe after the steaming *onsen*, the public baths. If you stay in a Japanese *ryokan*, a small traditional guest house, you may find a yukata left on the futon for your use. Generally these are not made to be taken with you when you leave. Yukata do not come with self belts, but usually are worn with a thickly woven webbed belt about two inches wide and six feet long. The belt is wrapped around the body and secured by tying or tucking in the ends.

Men's wave design yukata, possibly a dance costume. $70-90

Woman's bold graphic, made to look like shibori flowers with berries and branches. 1920s. $90-120

Katagami, a fabric screen, 1970s. Where there is a lot of open area, the yukata would be colored, usually with some shade of blue, and the stencil area is resisted, to show the base cloth color, usually white.

Woman's stencil dyed yukata. Bold pattern may be from the late Taisho period. $50-80

Robes showing the variety of blues utilized. They are called *ugari*, and the ones with *kanji*, lettering, are given to guests to use while visiting small hotels, called *ryokan*, or are worn after the bath. The geometric patterns are worn by men. The large blossom, divided diagonally by white and an indigo background, is a woman's robe. 1970s. $10-35, depending on condition

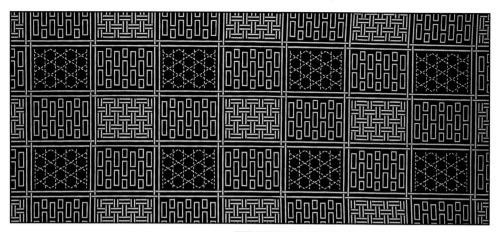

A screen of traditional geometric motifs in a repeat pattern.

Screen - stylized wisteria or paulownia design

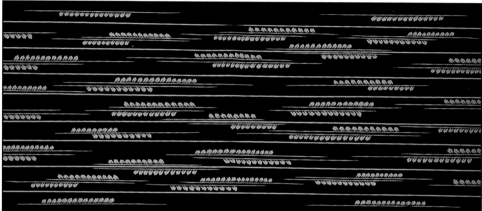

A packet of material that is enough for one yukata. The blue borders are unusual and would probably be incorporated into the design as a vertical element. The packet is called a *tan*, and is equivalent to about 12 yards. Traditional fabric widths are 14". This fabric is probably from the 1930s.

This shows a variety of new yukata that are popular overseas but, with the exception of the dragonfly motif, would not likely be worn in Japan. *From Arise.* $75-95 each

Contemporary yukata in short and long versions made for export and sized accordingly. The patterns update traditional motifs. *From Arise.* $75-95

3. Nagajuban-Undergarments

Nagajuban are shaped like a kimono and are worn as an undergarment close to the skin. For women, they are generally made from figured silk of white, red, pink or orange, or may also be decorated with *shibori*, tie dyed. As she walks and her kimono hem flips open, a glimpse of the under layer is revealed, and this makes a man think of the hue of the hidden skin below. The sleeves of a nagajuban are not sewn together at the sides, to permit the wearer to fit the kimono sleeve over it and to access what may be stored there, similar to a pocket.

Men's juban are similar, but of subdued colors of plain silk and often have images or surface design, such as shibori tie dyed patterns.

Back of a nagajuban pieced with over forty different materials that work together. Probably early early Showa period, very *iki* (stylish). Could be a combination of family kimono that had become too worn, and end of rolls, as two were found that were stenciled with stock numbers. 1930s. $200-300

This small piece of chirimen silk has a delicate yuzen design of ferns and flowers.

Taisho period woman's nagajuban of a highly sheened rinzu silk in red and white. Excellent condition. $150

Woman's nagajuban that is stained, but a keeper because of the techniques combined in it. Shibori koi with large air bubbles float amid supplementary weft lacquered threads of water eddies in black and silver. Sleeves and the waist were altered to accommodate a smaller person before the collar was reattached. The person who cleaned it also sewed characters in the collar, perhaps avowing that he was not responsible for the stains on the garment. Early Showa period. *Good Goods Collection.*

Very thin silk lined in red with a bold, all-over design not often seen. Family crests over clustered roses. Probably early 1920s. $75-125

Group of three nagajuban, all probably early 20th century. Linings are cotton with some rinzu and embroidery. Middle one is unusual as it has an embroidered collar, is shorter than the others, and has sleeves of chirimen silk. This could have been part of a dance costume. $80-150 each

Group of three nagajuban that, because of their good condition, could be made into a new garment. Probably these were worn by young girls, nine to twelve years old, under their kimono. The middle one is accented with shibori in three colors over rinzu silk. The daisy chain over alternating pink and white diagonals has been taken up twice inside, so would be much longer if let down. The third has water and flowers on a very soft crepe-like silk. Prices range from $40-60

Rinzu silk, shibori dyed on the diagonal, lined in cotton with rinzu silk collar. Early Showa period. $70-120

Unusual blue pieced garment, probably from the late 1930s or 1940s. Lace trim is on the inside of the sleeves and hem. Pale yellow cotton upper lining, with thin silk on the sleeves and hem. May also have been part of a dance costume. $90-120

Diaphanous dianthus flowers float down the red, peach and turquoise waters of this nagajuban. It is a summer weight under-kimono partially lined in the upper portion with pale silk. On the right, the ball design adds a playful touch to this young woman's undergarment, that is lined in red. 1920s. $50-70

A charming group of techniques and colors
are displayed. The triangular patterning of
yellow, green and purple shibori is done by
board clamping - *itajime*. The clouds of
purple and yellow are brush applied; this
pieced kimono has had many mends and
alterations. 1920s. $80-150

Detail of sleeve.

Front of a nagajuban pieced with over forty different materials that work together. Probably early early Showa period. Very *iki*, meaning stylish. This could be a combination of a family kimono that had become worn and ends of fabric rolls, as two sections were found that were stenciled with stock numbers. 1930s. $200-300

Another patchwork nagajuban made from a salesman's sample roll, 1920s-1930s. $150-200

Group of women's nagajuban. Two have surface designs of shibori technique. The teal and gray upper portion of the white one still has some raised portion from where the knots were tied. The white one in the middle has a very light overprint of a stylized wave design. It has been discreetly altered at the shoulders, and has glossy white embroidery on the collar. The green and white one is made to resemble horizontal wood grain. A simple explanation of how the design is made is that the fabric is wound around a pole, compressing it, and is held in place by wood rings before being placed in the dye bath.

Man's nagajuban with resisted area having a sumi-e painting. Gray silk, excellent condition. Late Showa period. $200-300

Darumas and poetry are icons of Zen Buddhism. Upon undertaking a task, a person is aware that he may fail seven times, only to succeed on the eighth. This juban is of fine quality silk lined in brown silk. Late Showa period. $200-300

Lightweight wool man's juban printed overall with parasols. Unusually large with blue raw silk collar. $200-300

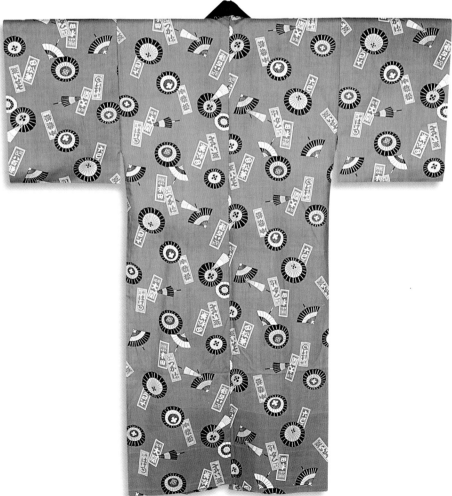

Fu dogs frolicking among bamboo stalks with thin white lines over the light brown background. Hand and machine stitching. 1970s. $150-250

Detail

Men's juban with *shotan* gourds on it. This printed design depicts a handy storage container for *sake*, rice wine. *"Kan pai"* is a traditional drinking salutation meaning "empty cup." 1960s. $130-150

Some men's juban and kimono have sleeves that are sewn under the arms. This one is open on both sides and shows a variety of musical instruments printed on the diagonal with alternating horizontal color bars, indicating that the former owner enjoyed the performing arts. $150-250

Mt. Fuji with *sake* barrels and yen coin design. Lined in silk, it probably was a rental juban. $250-300

Gray silk with hand painted scene of villages in snow. Note design of pine trees, *matsu*, at bottom. $150-200

Detail

Blue nagajuban. The wheels and diagonal design representing rain are Buddhist imagery for the wheel of life and the perseverance of water. $150-250

A juban that has been dyed by resisting some areas that were subsequently treated by sumi-e, a black ink wash expertly applied with a brush in a design of *darumas*, spirits who keep their eye on you as you complete tasks. $90-150

A representation of Mt. Fuji with people being carried in pallaquins and servants carrying their goods, possibly on a pilgrimage. Everything is executed in shibori, using capping off of areas to create the design. A very fancy juban, this probably was owned originally by a wealthy person. $400-500

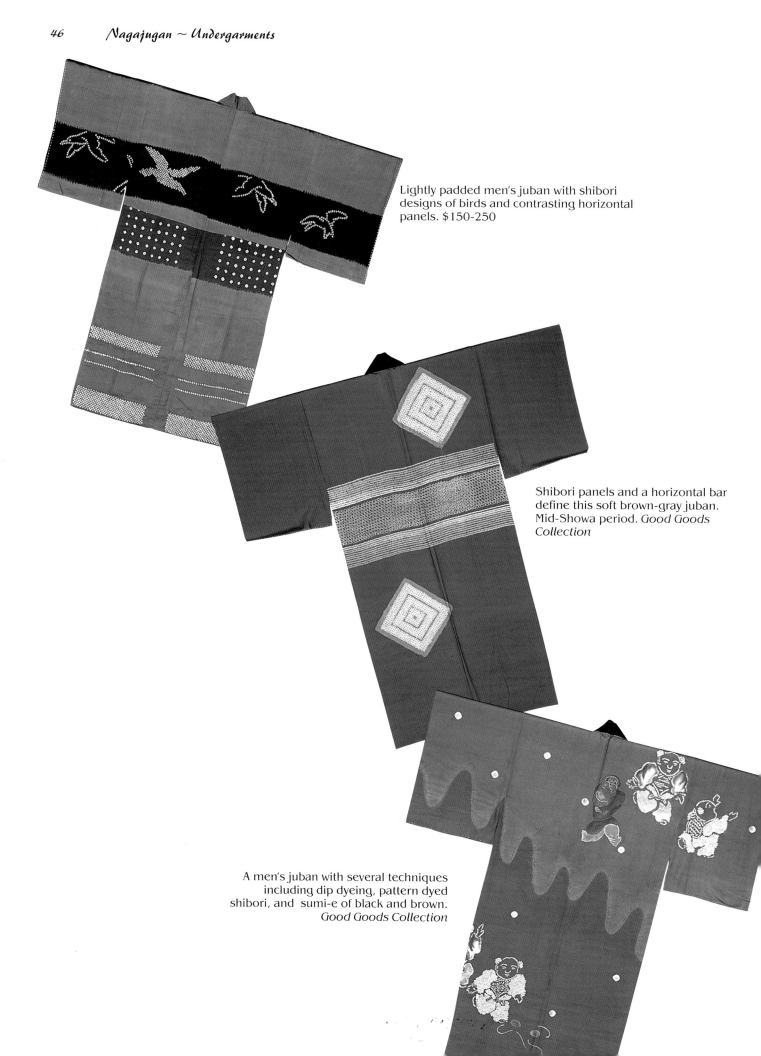

Lightly padded men's juban with shibori designs of birds and contrasting horizontal panels. $150-250

Shibori panels and a horizontal bar define this soft brown-gray juban. Mid-Showa period. *Good Goods Collection*

A men's juban with several techniques including dip dyeing, pattern dyed shibori, and sumi-e of black and brown. *Good Goods Collection*

4. Women's Kimono

Meisen ikat iridescent kimono with bubbles design. Lined in yellow at hem and sleeves, with red cotton upper. 1930-1940s. *Good Goods Collection*

The Japanese call their traditional forms of clothing *wafuku*, and the shape we call kimono started out being a *kosode*, referring to the small opening of the sleeve. Sleeve length is very important in kimono. A young woman wears the longest sleeve, *ofurisode*, because it will swing and be flirtatious when she walks. She wears *furisode* length at the ceremony of nineteen years of age. As she grows older and marries, ithe sleeve gets shortened to *kosode* length, reflecting her altered station in life.

Westerners generally wear these garments, originally made to be elegantly borne upon the body, without a thought to the original protocol. That is a good thing, because few westerners would have the patience, and fewer still the build, to carry off the intended elegance.

When westerners put on a kimono, they notice that the gown drapes on the floor. This happens because the proper way of wearing a kimono is to make a fold at the waist and secure it so that it falls precisely to the ankle. The sleeve is meant to come to the wrist. In Japan today, most women must attend schools to find out how to put on and wear kimono properly, since they have few occasions to practice this ancient art of dress.

During the twentieth century, when Japanese women entered the work force, kimono became slightly more practical and easier to wear. Meisen ikat became a popular fabric for kimono as it was simpler to clean and care for, and more durable, too.

For doing errands such as shopping or casual visiting, a *fudangi* was worn. This could be a striped kimono or one with little decoration. For festive occasions or formal visits, *homongi* made of better quality silk with more detailing were necessary.

Motifs

Although motifs in nature are always present on Japanese garments, the way of interpreting them is subject to changes in tastes and trends. Floral images are often depicted, such as the chrysanthemum, representing the Emperor, and the peony, which is adapted from Chinese culture. *Sho-chiku bai* motif is pine, bamboo, plum (three friends) for fortitude and faith. Many other motifs appear frequently, including the seven autumn grasses, and the swallows of spring. Cranes are considered a wish for a thousand years of life, and everyday items, such as cartwheels, basket weaves and fans, are used frequently in designs because their shapes are pleasing. Shinto and Buddhist icons also appear: the swastika represents the wheel of life, yin-yang is a pre-historic symbol, and thickly wound rope is often found at Shinto shrines and on kimono.

Detail of maroon kimono with fan
rinzu and yuzen mums

Detail of tsukesage kimono
sleeve design

Meisen geometric design with contrasting warp and weft threads, giving a shimmering effect. Lined in yellow cotton at hem and sleeves with red cotton upper; probably early Early Showa period. $120-$150
Good Goods Collection

Rinzu background of checkerboard design, with showy peonies in red and silver gray; lined with turquoise silk at hem and sleeves and red silk above. $110-160

Fine quality silk with woven medallions of floral design lined entirely in red. Late Showa period. $90-120

This detail of a kimono design gives the illusion of shibori flowers and uses a rinzu to create diagonals.

June Colburn layered silk from solid maroon kimono, sewed them together, and slashed open the areas between the rows of stitching to create this versatile jacket.

The contrast of black and white makes this simple sha style
of woven silk an almost incandescent kimono decorated with
dragonflies and woven baskets. $300-400

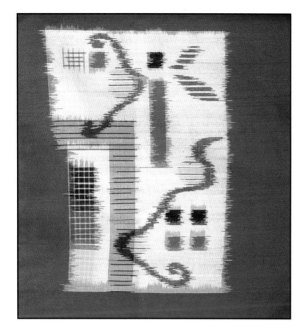

Ikat design of a stylized dragonfly.

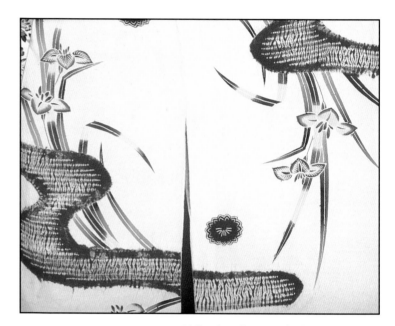

Shibori and yuzen dyeing.

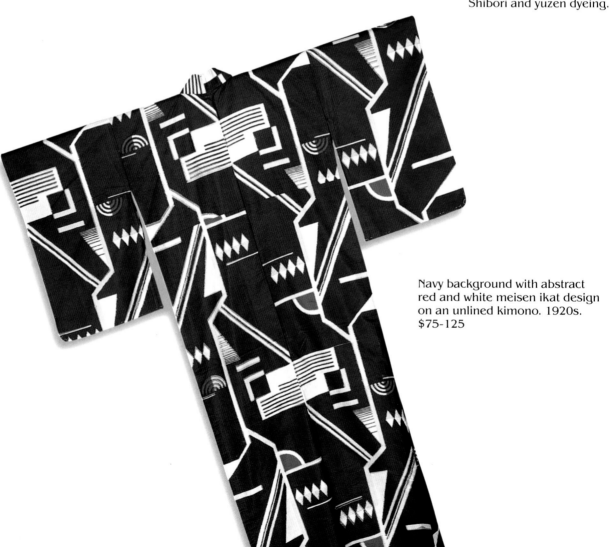

Navy background with abstract
red and white meisen ikat design
on an unlined kimono. 1920s.
$75-125

Group of three kimono used for going out to do everyday errands. Yellow one has *habane* design, resembling arrow quills. Stripes are very popular in Japanese clothes, though it is not what people usually think of in relation to their clothing. 1950-1960s. $50-70

Other examples of striped and arrow designed kimono for shopping and everyday wear. Mid-century. $60-90

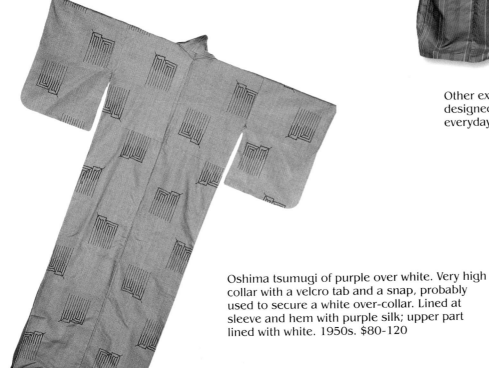

Oshima tsumugi of purple over white. Very high collar with a velcro tab and a snap, probably used to secure a white over-collar. Lined at sleeve and hem with purple silk; upper part lined with white. 1950s. $80-120

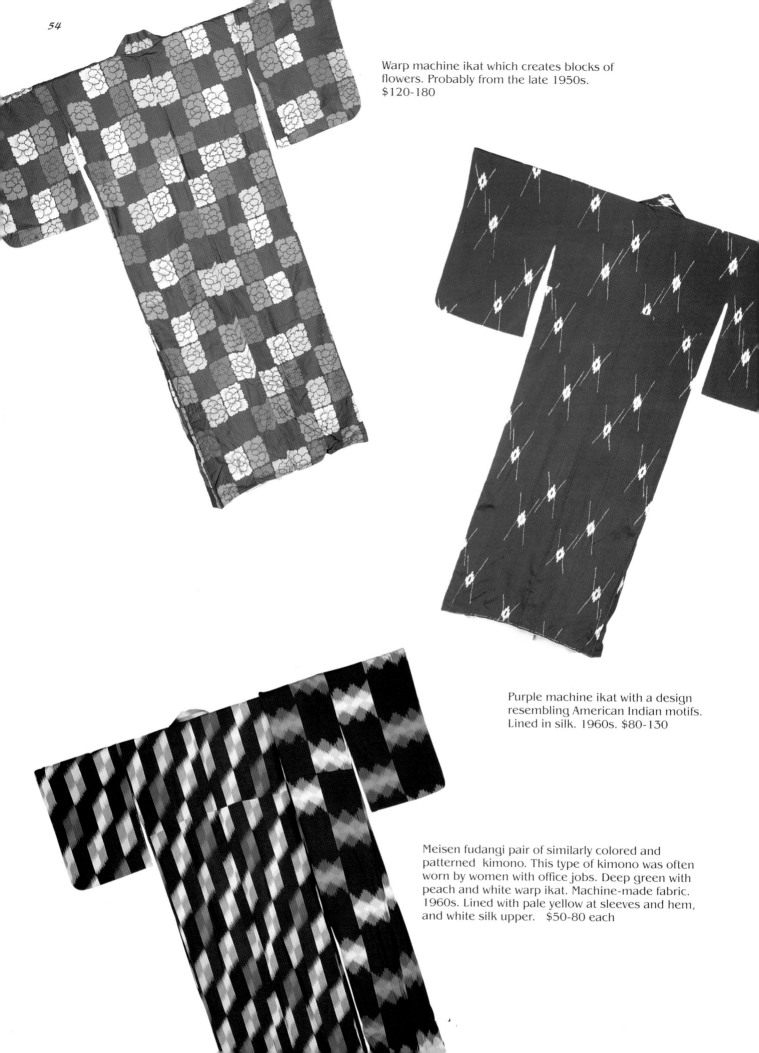

Warp machine ikat which creates blocks of flowers. Probably from the late 1950s. $120-180

Purple machine ikat with a design resembling American Indian motifs. Lined in silk. 1960s. $80-130

Meisen fudangi pair of similarly colored and patterned kimono. This type of kimono was often worn by women with office jobs. Deep green with peach and white warp ikat. Machine-made fabric. 1960s. Lined with pale yellow at sleeves and hem, and white silk upper. $50-80 each

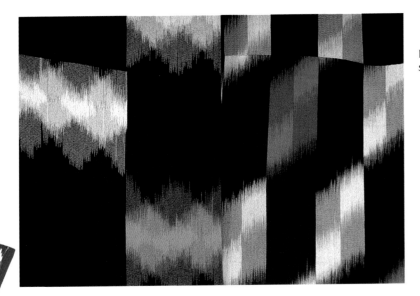

Detail of the two patterns side by side; don't stare at this too long, dizziness might occur.

A pair of fudangi kimono of the same tonal colors and similar design. Both have warp ikat designs, probably machine made of silk with silk linings. Late Showa period, 1960s. Worn at home by a woman of 30 to 40 years of age. $60-80 each

Machine ikat pattern of white and red on navy blue. Lined at sleeves and hem with rust colored silk with white upper. 1950-1960s. $60-90

Although at first glance this is a very straightforward design, being fairly geometric, it could be a small view of a dragonfly over a field. Whimsical ikat design lined in cotton. $60-90

Red and white with subtle gray ikat in crosshatch pattern. Mid-Showa period. Unlined. *Good Goods Collection*

Warp and weft ikat on brick colored silk lined with white cotton. Possibly made on a machine, post-World War II. $80-120

Woman's meisen ikat kimono with geometric design lined in peach silk at the sleeves and hem with red cotton upper. 1930s. $120-160

Fudangi meisen woven unlined kimono of black background with trees. 1960s. $100-150

Hitoe of the Taisho period with star shaped leaves done by stencil design in gold, silver and pink; worn in summer months. $120-150

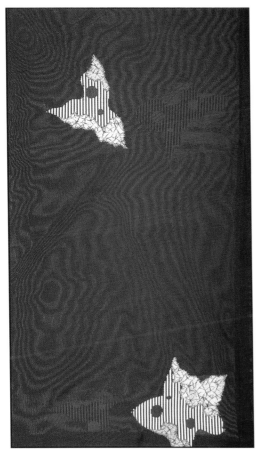

Detail of sleeve showing the delicate weave of the garment. A white nagajuban would have been worn underneath.

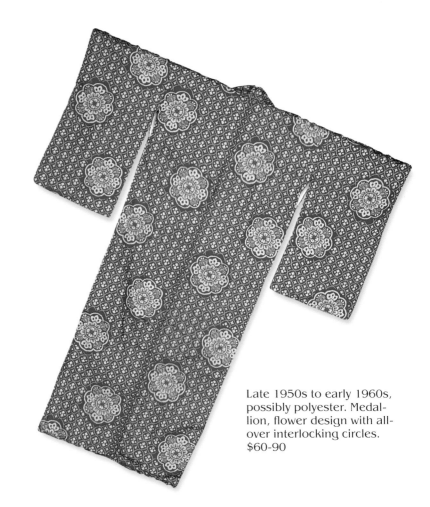

Late 1950s to early 1960s, possibly polyester. Medallion, flower design with all-over interlocking circles. $60-90

Red background with wavy stripes showcase the yellow bamboo that is woven into the surface using a supplementary weft weaving technique. Maroon at hem and sleeves, with red upper. 1940 to 1950s. $150-250

Iridescent sheen achieved by contrasting warp and weft threads. Medallions of flowers in ikat pattern. $120-180

An ikat that resembles a plaid in red, navy and yellow. Mid-Showa period. $120-180

Two kimono of medium weight silk with linings of silk at the sleeves and hem and cotton upper, for wearing at home by an older woman. The overall floral one has a silvery cast to it and a jaunty trim of lace at the sleeve. $120-180 each

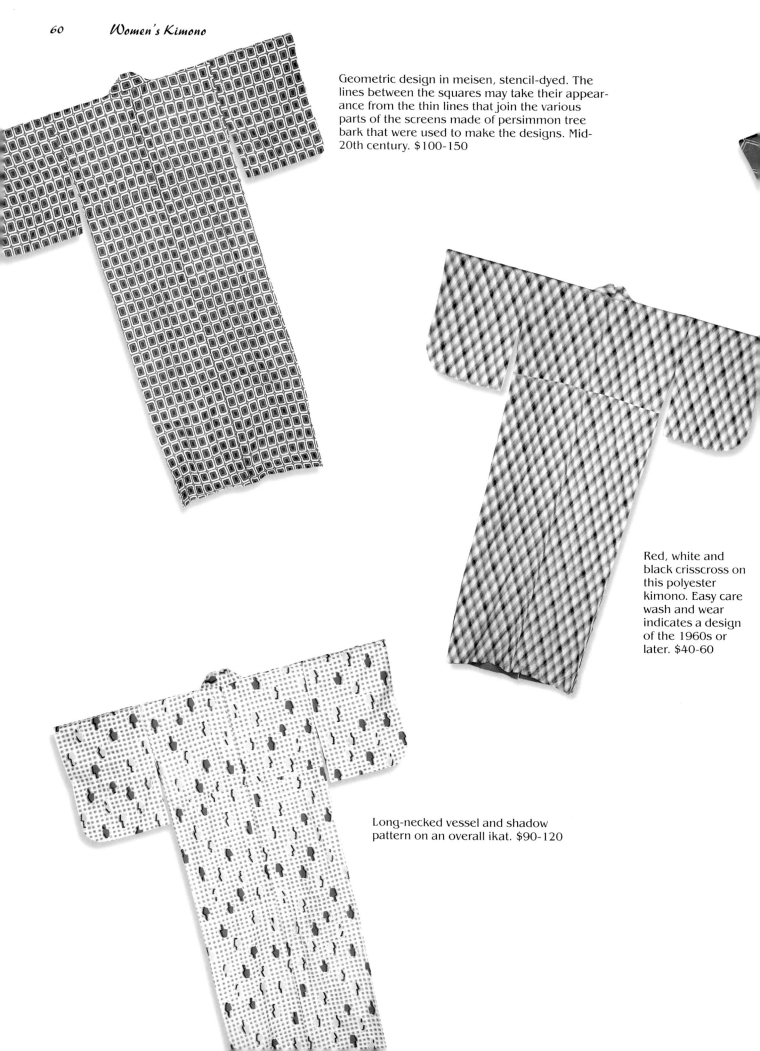

Geometric design in meisen, stencil-dyed. The lines between the squares may take their appearance from the thin lines that join the various parts of the screens made of persimmon tree bark that were used to make the designs. Mid-20th century. $100-150

Red, white and black crisscross on this polyester kimono. Easy care wash and wear indicates a design of the 1960s or later. $40-60

Long-necked vessel and shadow pattern on an overall ikat. $90-120

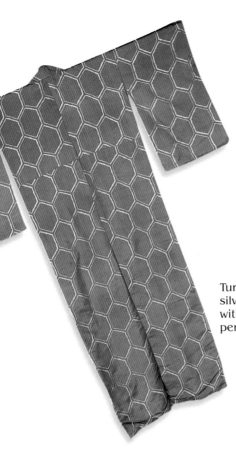

Deep green silk with medium length sleeves. Diagonal design resembling wood grain. This is a *chokochokogi*, a colloquial term for an everyday kimono. 1960s. Lined at sleeves and hem with black, with red silk upper. $110-140

Turtle shell design in maroon and silver gray. Lightweight and lined with three kinds of silk. Late Showa period. $80-120

Four very different ikats from the early part of the century.

Woman's summer kimono with sleeves that have been taken up, possibly to indicate her change in status from being a single to a married woman. Unlined. $60-90

Detail of image on previous page; note white weft thread, about every quarter inch, in additional to multi-colored image. Some areas appear weft and warp, others weft only. *Good Goods Collection*

The front of a kimono, with typical lining coloration. The outside is an iridescent ikat, in a geometric diamond pattern. 1950-1960s. $120-180

Meisen *habane* (arrow feather) design. Red in the weft and purple in the warp threads make for an iridescent sheen to the silk, probably late 1920s. Partly lined in red, with silk at the sleeves and cotton at the hem. Excellent condition. $120-180

Iridescent meisen ikat, possibly 1940s to 1950s.

Meisen ikat kimono with iridescent sheen. *Good Goods Collection*

A geisha in training, probably between fifteen and nineteen years old, dances to the music of a *shamisen*. The hairstyles and red collar, called *mai-ko*, are worn by an understudy and help to identify the image. Early twentieth century.

Kimono of black silk with orange yuzen flowers accented with gold. Rust color lining at hem and sleeves, with white above. Late Showa period. $150 -200.

Modern crosshatched printed design resembling a fence or screen in green with peach. Could be a silk/rayon combination, a washable kimono. Probably a visiting kimono. Late Showa period, 1960-1970s. $80-120

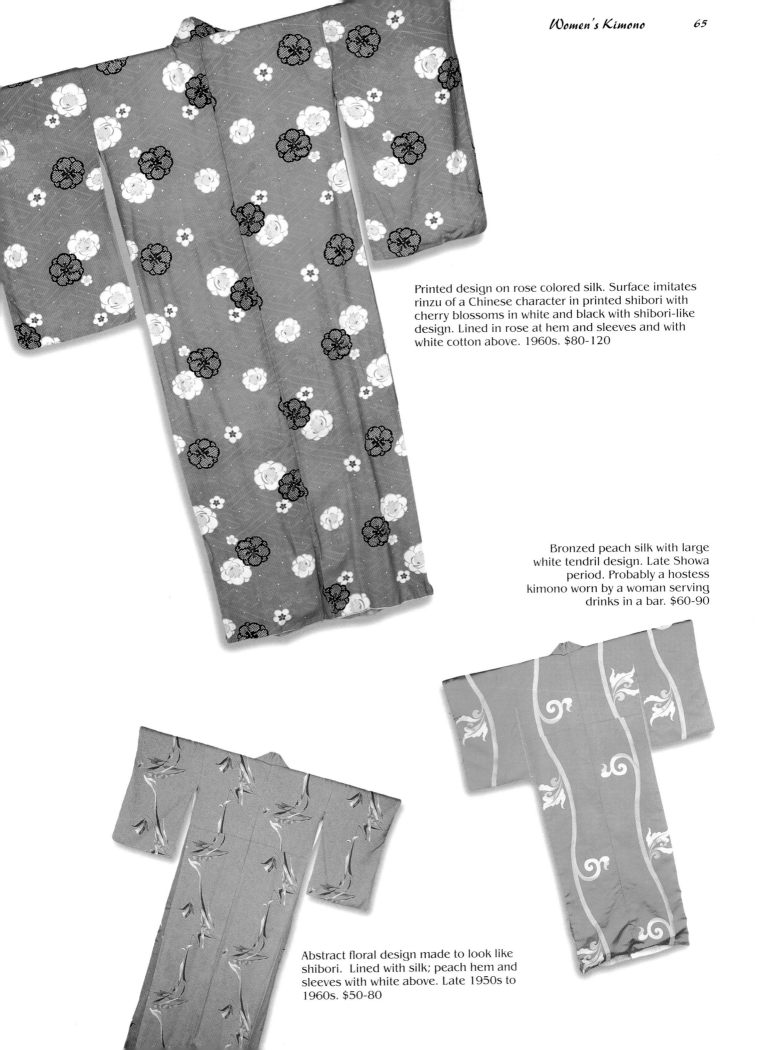

Printed design on rose colored silk. Surface imitates rinzu of a Chinese character in printed shibori with cherry blossoms in white and black with shibori-like design. Lined in rose at hem and sleeves and with white cotton above. 1960s. $80-120

Bronzed peach silk with large white tendril design. Late Showa period. Probably a hostess kimono worn by a woman serving drinks in a bar. $60-90

Abstract floral design made to look like shibori. Lined with silk; peach hem and sleeves with white above. Late 1950s to 1960s. $50-80

Shown open to reveal the totality of the design, this visiting kimono has a design of blossoming branches and colorful chrysanthemums. It is yuzen painted on a background of deep red and pale pink for dramatic effect. One delicately embroidered mon on the back is in gold thread. Some spotting, but generally good condition. 1940s. $250-350

Detail of design

Orange and white interlocking circles on pebbly finished rinzu silk; lined at sleeves and hem with yellow silk. 1970s. $220-270

Stylized irises are strewn over this pale pink informal visiting kimono. 1960s. $50-80

Open weave, mint green, unlined summer kimono with fuschia dyed accents for everyday wear. Possibly a light wool. 1960s. $80-120

Pale pinks and hand-drawn naive flowers grace this silken *tsukesage* kimono that may have been worn by a geisha. The design is on the back, down the left front, and on the right hem and sleeve. Lined with white silk, edged in pink. Late Showa period. Marred by a stain on the front, this kimono would sell for about $60-90.

Peonies with silver centers, lined with
white and pink; excellent condition.
Late Showa period. $120-170

Red and white mums on a
navy field and lined with
pink and red; excellent
condition. A *nagagi*, worn
for visiting. Late Showa
period. $90-140

Black background with red, gold, and
silver imitation of supplementary weft
lacquered thread work. Very good condition. $120-150

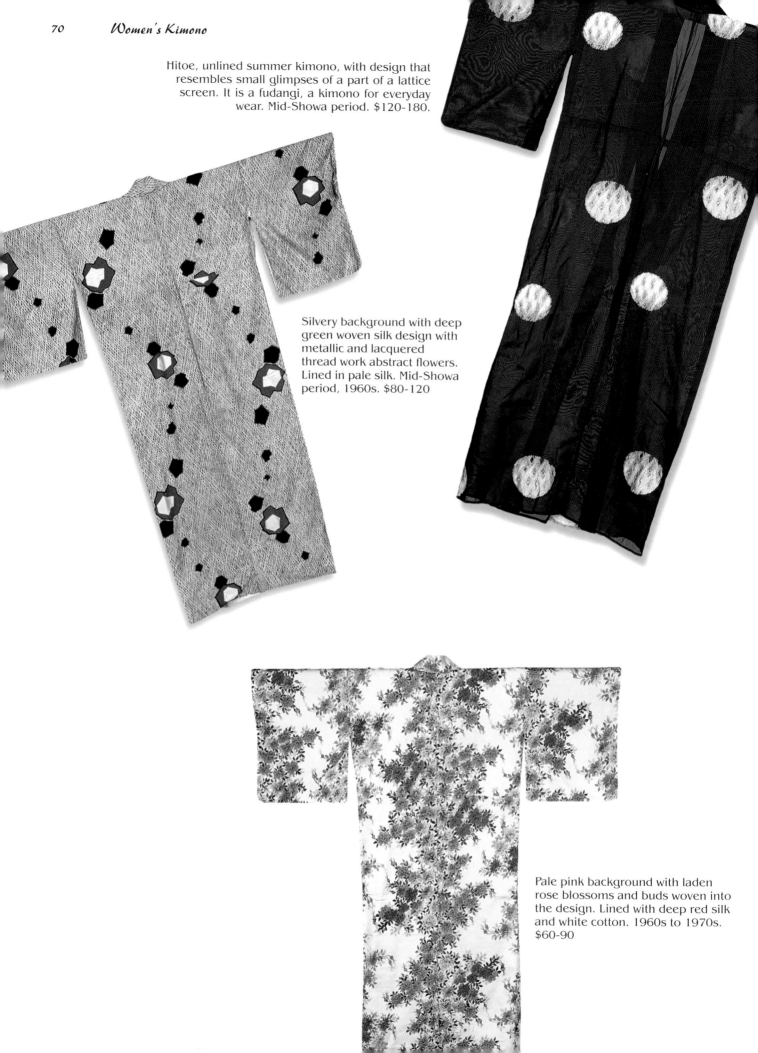

Hitoe, unlined summer kimono, with design that resembles small glimpses of a part of a lattice screen. It is a fudangi, a kimono for everyday wear. Mid-Showa period. $120-180.

Silvery background with deep green woven silk design with metallic and lacquered thread work abstract flowers. Lined in pale silk. Mid-Showa period, 1960s. $80-120

Pale pink background with laden rose blossoms and buds woven into the design. Lined with deep red silk and white cotton. 1960s to 1970s. $60-90

Non-silk kimono, maybe wool. Metallic row of threads approximately every twenty rows horizontally make for an interesting catch of light when the fabric moves. Printed modern design. 1960 to 1970s. $50-70

Maroon with very thin black stripes and abstract design woven into the cloth. Lined entirely in red. Early Showa period, around the 1930s. $75-125.

Heavy deep red silk kimono
with supplementary weft
lacquered thread work. Lined
in silk. 1920s. $250-350

Fudangi kimono in subdued colors but with a lively flower pattern. The alternating up-and-down view of the pattern is a recurring theme in Japanese design. Outer not silk; inner silk with some spotting. Late Showa period. Value reflects condition. $60-90

Detail of design

Nagagi, visiting kimono of maroon silk with silver rosebud design lined in pink at the sleeves and hem, with white upper. 1950 to 1960s. $80-120

Left: Detail of fan design on kimono sleeve.

Right: Detail of sleeve with floral spray.

Black with magenta cherry blossoms and chrysanthemums design. Late Showa period. Lined with copper colored silk at sleeves and hem, with red above. $100-180

Understated but a special kimono. Background is maroon with blue wood grain pattern, followed next by a stenciled application of pine branches and needles overall.   Next a hand painted application of yellow pollen is tipped onto the center of each cluster. The lining has raw silk of spring green color at the hem and is pieced with some printed cotton above. 1940s. $120-180

Delicate branches in bloom are reproduced in this machine-made design.

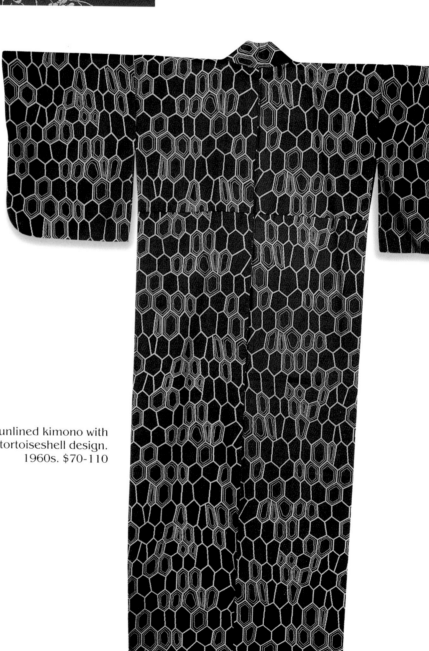

Black unlined kimono with woven blue tortoiseshell design. 1960s. $70-110

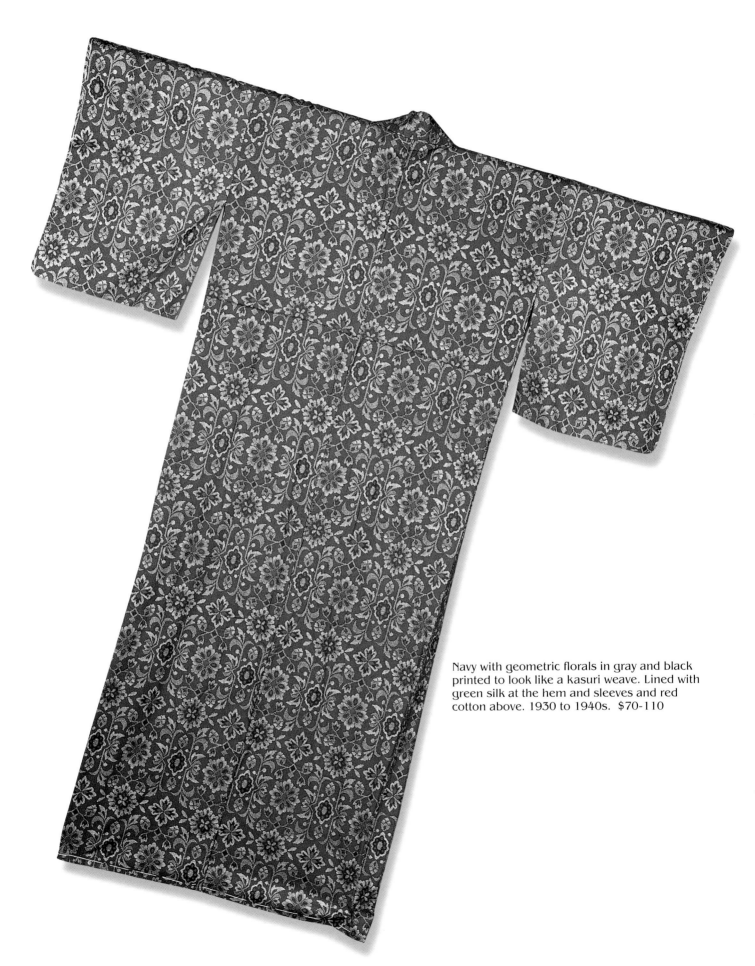

Navy with geometric florals in gray and black printed to look like a kasuri weave. Lined with green silk at the hem and sleeves and red cotton above. 1930 to 1940s. $70-110

Rinzu silk of tiny dots with blue and pink flowers and gold embroidery accents cascading over the kimono. White silk lining with green *bokashi* dip-dyeing at the sleeves and hem. Mid-Showa period, 1950s. $75-90

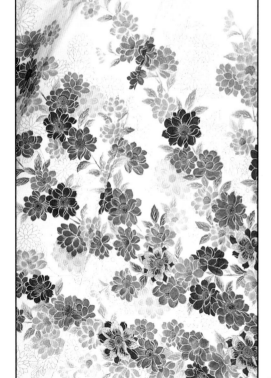

Detail of design

Tsukesage kimono of pale gray with woven flower design. Lined with white silk upper, and pale gray at hem and sleeves. Possibly late 1950s. $90-150

Black with metallic pink peacock feathers all-over design. Lined on sleeves and hem with rust; white silk upper. This type of shiny material could have been worn by a hostess in a bar. 1970s. $80-120

A hostess style kimono in black with all-over silver flower design with blue accents. 1970s. $60-90

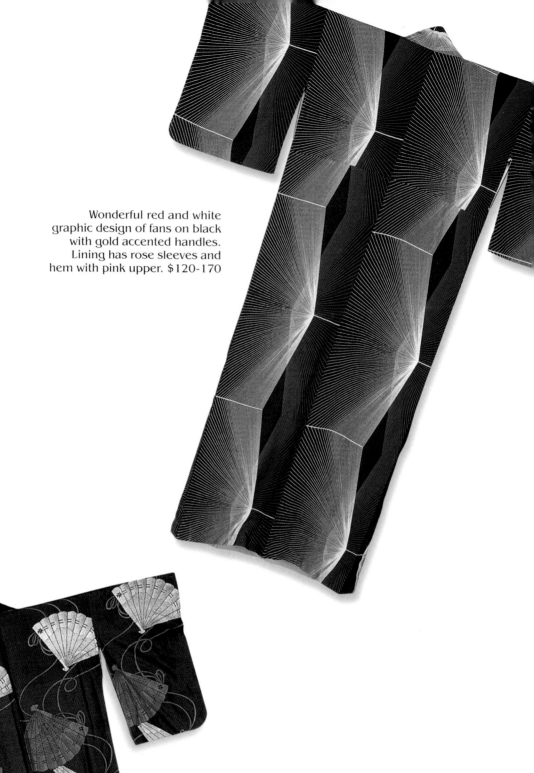

Wonderful red and white
graphic design of fans on black
with gold accented handles.
Lining has rose sleeves and
hem with pink upper. $120-170

Black raw silk with fans and cords printed
to look like lacquer. Cotton lining. 1950s
to 1960s. $120-150

Homongi kimono for special
occasion visiting. *Ji gara*,
another type of figured silk, of
rich maroon color with
chrysanthemums and yellow
geometric diagonal. One mon
on center of back. Unusual
embroidery detailing on
flowers of cross hatched and
metallic multi-olored and
silver threads. Lined in red
silk. Early Showa period.
$400-600

White rinzu of chryanthemums on surface with yuzen design of various flowers and stylized vertical waves in red and yellow with pink; looks quirky, but it works! 1960s. $120-180

Furisode, medium long-sleeved kimono. Beautiful yuzen, dip dyeing, of water and gold embroidery make the parts of this kimono greater than the whole. The lining is spotted, possibly from the metallic threads. 1960s. $75-125

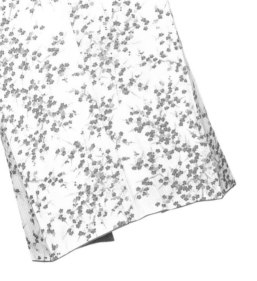

Komon nagagi, an all-over design on a more formal visiting kimono. Pale yellow background with budding cherry blossoms. Springtime kimono in very good condition. 1960s, late Showa period. $240-300

Detail of pattern.

Nagagi kimono of *bi jin ga,* beautiful women romanticized in the floating world, glimpsed through small sections of screens. Muted colors but very striking design. Printed pattern. Lined entirely in white with accents at hem and sleeves of flowing sage green called bokashi. Delightful. From the 1960s. $400-500

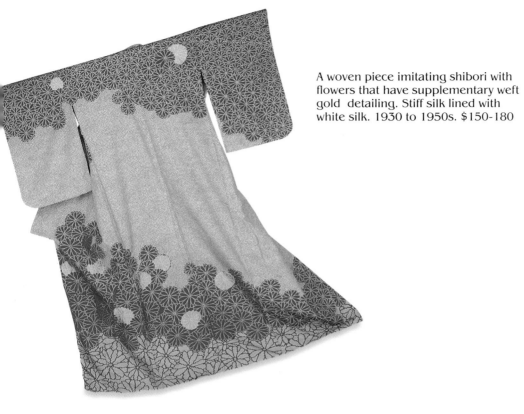

A woven piece imitating shibori with flowers that have supplementary weft gold detailing. Stiff silk lined with white silk. 1930 to 1950s. $150-180

Orange kimono with elaborate spider chrysanthemum design. Gold surihaku over yuzen. 1950s. $400-475

Soft silk with rinzu of vertical stripes,
machine produced effect of yuzen accented
with red, yellow, peach and gray stylized
bamboo leaves. Surihaku, gold painting, on
the edges of the leaves. Hem and sleeves
lined in pink silk; upper in red. 1960 to
1970s. $160-200

Detail of leaves and
surihaku.

Gray *tsumungi* silk with yuzen design of clouds and cherry blossoms with gold surihaku leaf application for accents. Lined with pink silk at hem and sleeves. 1940s. $230-280

Peach colored silk with bamboo and chrysanthemum printed design. Lined with peach silk at hem and sleeves and white cotton above. 1930s to 1940s. $120-160

Delicate ikat woven design of
lilac with hexagonal floral details.
This is a hitoe, an unlined
summer kimono. Good condition. $90-140

Hitoe, unlined summer kimono, of *ro* silk with silver accents; subtly dyed areas, bokashi, of burnt orange and fan and flowers in lilac. 1960s. *Good Goods Collection*.

Detail of kimono.

Beautiful purple homongi, visiting kimono, with squares of stylized chrysanthemums that are yuzen, rice paste resist painted with surihaku, gold accents. Lined in shades of pink silk. Excellent condition. 1940s. $250-300

Deep green kimono with gold surihaku leaf accents and printed design of stylized flowers. It is lined at the sleeves and hem with rust colored silk and a pale pink cotton upper. Late 1950s to the early 1960s. $100-150

Front view of a lovely nagagi kimono probably from the 1930s to 1940s. Gray rinzu background with shibori purple clouds and yuzen circles of colorful flowers. Lined at hem and sleeves with gold silk and red upper. Has been worn quite a bit, therefore has a mark on the center of back, but for display it could be covered with an obi or sewn to conceal the mark. Price reflects condition $200-300

Blue-green background and design of bamboo and clouds on a fall or winter kimono that would have been worn by a mature woman. Sleeves and hem lined in dusty mauve silk with pale yellow upper. $100-150

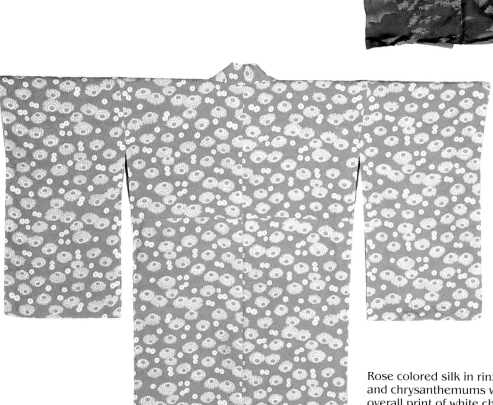

Rose colored silk in rinzu with Chinese characters and chrysanthemums woven into the silk and an overall print of white chrysanthemums edged in gray. Lined in peach silk at hem and sleeves with red silk upper. Late Showa period. $150-200

Tsukesage style of kimono where the pattern ascends from the hem to the sleeve. Deep pink color with floral arrangements of traditional flowers. Could be yuzen. Showa period, probably early 1970s. $350-400

Detail of kimono

Pink background with tiny white dots in half wave pattern and clusters of white flowers in an overall pattern grace this springtime visiting kimono. 1960s. $80-120

Burnt orange rinzu of pine needles with simulated shibori design of fans yuzen dyed overall. Excellent condition. Machine printed. 1970s, late Showa period. $360-450

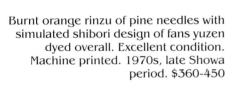

Ecru white rinzu silk with clouds, yuzen stencils of various colored bamboo and couched threads on left front of this fudangi, a visiting kimono. Very old traditional design motif. Very good condition. Late Showa period. $300-350

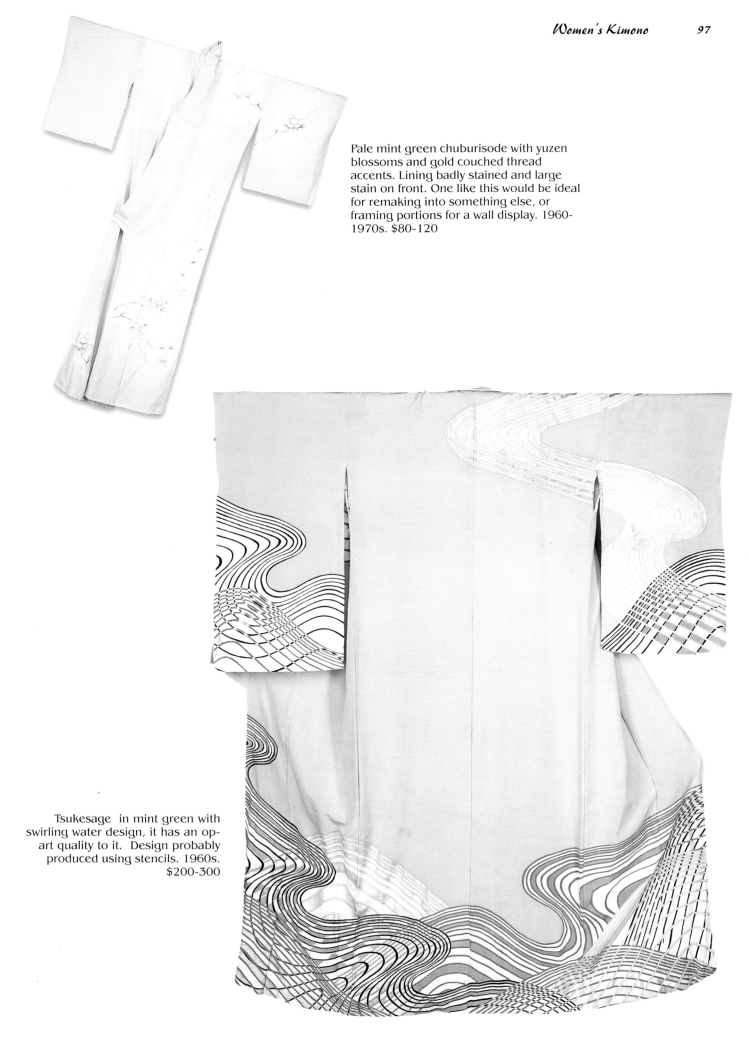

Pale mint green chuburisode with yuzen blossoms and gold couched thread accents. Lining badly stained and large stain on front. One like this would be ideal for remaking into something else, or framing portions for a wall display. 1960-1970s. $80-120

Tsukesage in mint green with swirling water design, it has an op-art quality to it. Design probably produced using stencils. 1960s. $200-300

Opposite page:
Green tsukesage kimono with yuzen painted gourds with flowers inside them. Three family crests appear, meaning it is not the most formal style but also not a regular visiting kimono. Lined in green silk at the hem and sleeves with red silk upper. Early Showa period. $1200-1500

Festive kimono with shibori detailing of waves and fans. The impression of wearing an obi can be noticed. Showa period, 1970s. $300-400

Tsukesage kimono in orange chirimin-like silk with insets of colorful chrysanthemums on beige background, worn in autumn or spring. 1940 to1950s. $200-350

Ro, silk that is woven in horizontal lines, hitoe, an unlined kimono worn in summer, of soft green with hand painted dianthus, pines, and silver fishing nets. Modern design, probably 1960s to 1970s. Three family crests appear. *Good Goods Collection.*

Detail of the ro weave and the family crest. The area for the design was resisted out and the mon crest drawn in with a steady hand and black ink.

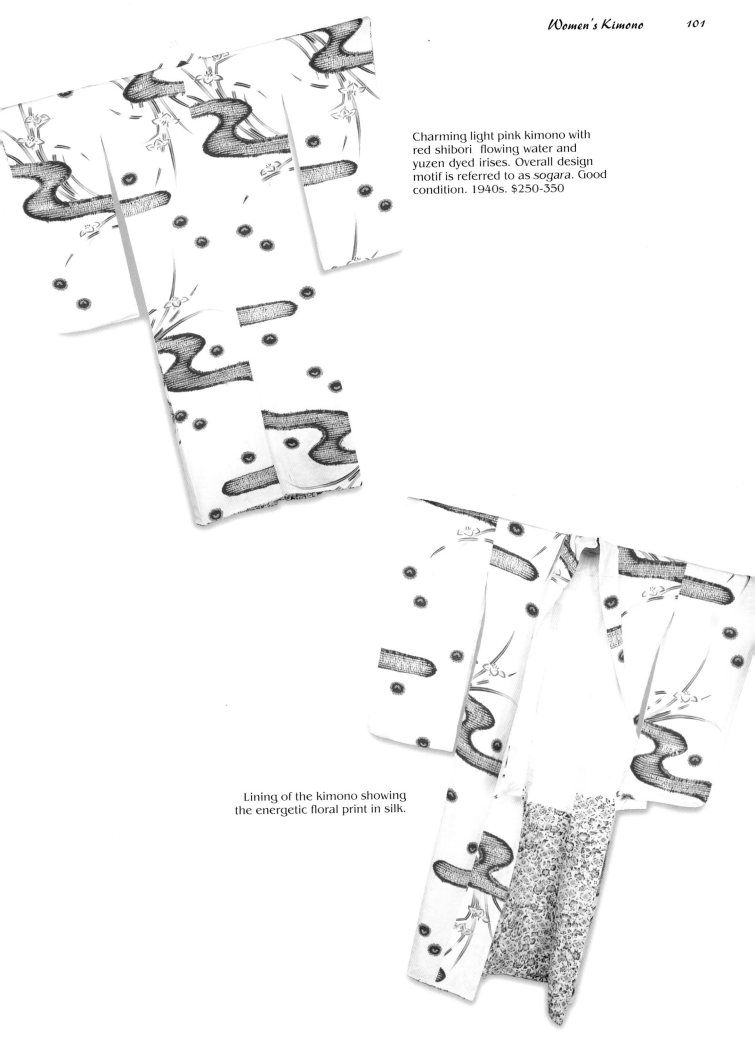

Charming light pink kimono with red shibori flowing water and yuzen dyed irises. Overall design motif is referred to as *sogara*. Good condition. 1940s. $250-350

Lining of the kimono showing the energetic floral print in silk.

5. Tomesode ~ Kimono for Formal Occasions

A *tomesode* (toe-may-so-day), the most formal kimono a woman would wear, bears her family's *mon*, or family crest. The use of five family crests on her kimono indicates the most formal garment, with two at the front sleeves, two on the back of the sleeve, and one on the center seam. Three crests only across the back indicates a slightly less formal kimono. The crests are produced by hand drawing the delicate image in a resisted area. The hem of the tomesode is decorated with designs that are elegant and full of auspicious images. Tomesode are often worn by family members of both the bride and the groom at a wedding ceremony.

Detail of embroidery and painted design.

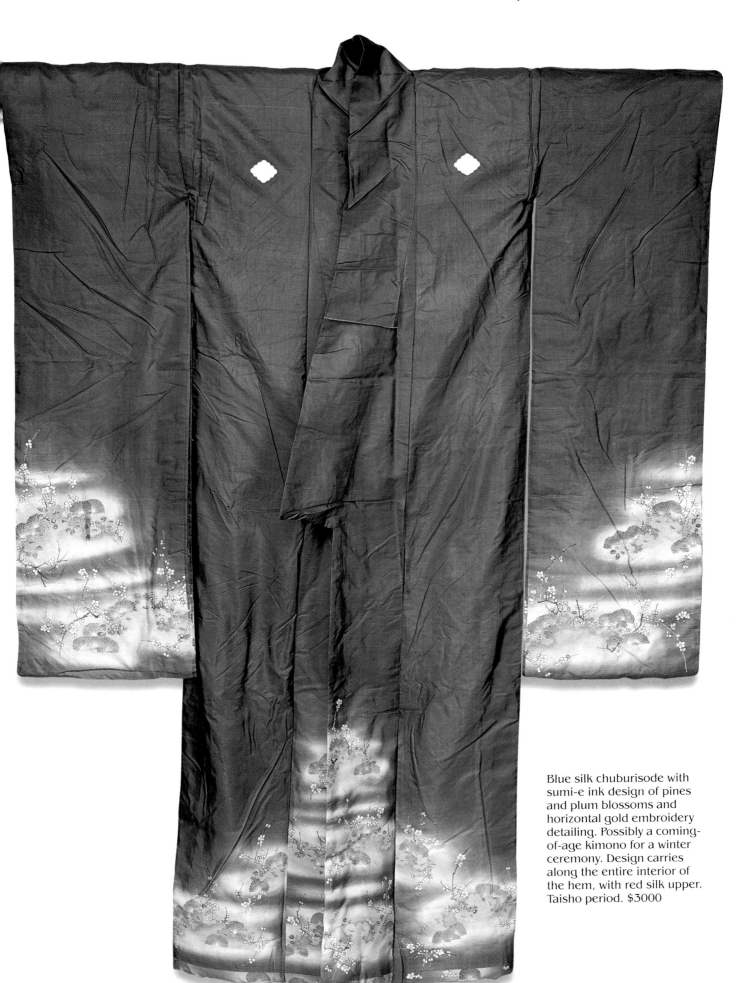

Blue silk chuburisode with sumi-e ink design of pines and plum blossoms and horizontal gold embroidery detailing. Possibly a coming-of-age kimono for a winter ceremony. Design carries along the entire interior of the hem, with red silk upper. Taisho period. $3000

Mt. Fuji in the far distance with gift carts and open flowers delicately painted using the yuzen technique. Design continues on the inside at the hem. Lined in red silk in upper body and sleeves. Taisho period. $500-700

Design closeup.

Tomesode with yuzen hem decoration of pine needles and cranes, water, bamboo and cherry blossoms. Some embroidered details include a crest of cranes, center of blossoms, and pine pollen. Lined entirely in white with sewn-in inner collar of chirimen silk. Mon are covered in tissue paper, meaning this could be a new kimono made for a particular family but was never completed. $250-300

Pines and waves design. Photo suggests a way to display the kimono that reveals how the image connects around the robe. Yuzen of chirimen silk with intact surihaku painting. Design continues on the inside, and the upper is lined in ivory silk. $200-300

This shows the back of a 1960s tomesode with embroidered flowers and low fence design with surihaku, gold leaf technique. Lining of white silk in two layers. $150-200

A variety of elegant objects — including tea containers wrapped in silk, vases, *inro* (a small container worn on a kimono near the obi)— that symbolize those given to a wedding couple appear in shades of orange and gold (for richness) with couched threads and resisted cloud-like areas. $250-300

The Buddhist symbol of a lotus in a pool surrounds the inner and outer sides of this tomesode kimono. Gold and silver surihaku, as well as couching of gold and multicolor threads and tiny accent embroidery in the center of the flowers are ornamental. Late Showa period. $300-350

Lining of tomesode.

Couched thread work of pines makes a dramatic statement on the hem of this tomesode. Lined in white. Late Showa period. $150-175.
Narrow obi of gold and white with an interlocking letter design. These particular pieces, however, would not be worn together, as the designs, to a Japanese person's eye, are not suited to each other. $120-150

Another variation of pines and waves in delicate shades of blue and purple. Late Showa period. $250-300

The pattern wraps around the kimono at the hem on this homongi, a fancy visiting kimono. It could have been worn to a wedding ceremony by someone other than the family members. Rose colored rinzu silk with leaf and mum pattern, it has areas that have been resisted to form clouds, then the hem has yuzen flowers and a cart design with embroidered details in the flowers. One delicately stitched mon appears in the center of the back. Taisho period. $2000-2500

Detail of the design.

A rose colored homongi kimono with rose rinzu. Since roses are not cultivated in Japan, their appearance here places this kimono in the early Taisho period when influence from the Western world was apparent and imagery not formerly seen was introduced into Japanese iconography. The hem design shows a basket and large flowers. Most are yuzen, but one or two are over-painted in white, possibly done sometime after the garment was originally designed. Embroidery detailing includes the basket weave stitch as well as couching. 1920s to 1930s. $2000-2500

"Tomesode Fan" wall quilt by June Colburn. The yuzen design of the hem of this garment lends itself so well to an adaptation like this, when the garment is damaged or you want to be creative in a way to display and preserve the textile. The cord of the fan is dimensional, projecting slightly out from the surface.

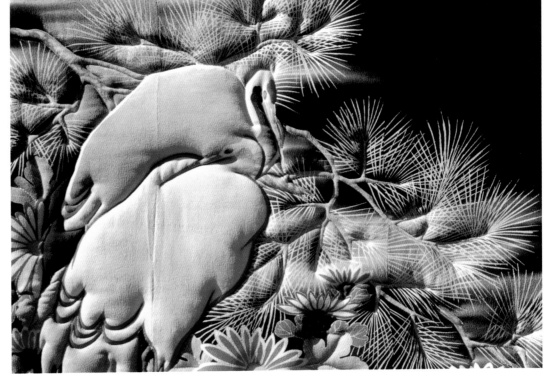

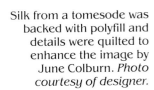

Silk from a tomesode was backed with polyfill and details were quilted to enhance the image by June Colburn. *Photo courtesy of designer.*

A box for the storage of tea, decorated by June Colburn, utilizes the bottom of a tomesode kimono to good effect. *Photo courtesy of designer.*

6. The Obi and Accessories

Obi (oh-be) are long and wide stiff silk wide sashes used to secure the kimono at the topmost layer. There's over 100 ways to tie them, according to the season, a woman's age or the formality of the event being attended. A full study of the various weaving techniques and styles of obi is beyond the scope of this book. Here we are more concerned with their beauty and design. There are basically two types of obi: one that is fourteen inches wide and about fourteen feet long, generally called a *maru* obi, and a Nagoya obi, from the city of the same name, that has about three feet of full width, which makes the bow, and the rest folded in half and stitched, to wrap around the body. There are also clip on obi, for people in a real rush.

The various parts of a kimono ensemble are held together with different sashes and ties. *Obi age* and *obi jime* are included in this section. There is an old saying that the obi symbolizes Japan's beauty. While to westerners the kimono is the important attire, the obi is most important to the Japanese.

Accessories

Collar covers are another separate part of the kimono costume that bear special notice. They can be cleaned easily without having to clean the entire garment.

Tabi socks are made with the large toe separated from the other toes so that *zori* or *getta* sandals can be more easily worn.

Purses, wallets, hair combs, *netsuke*, and *inro* all complete the costume.

This pillow has pieced corners and a center panel from a brocade obi. Some maru obi are very useful for production sewers, yielding almost 28 feet of material, with the image repeating about every one-and-a-half to two feet. *Pillow and photo by June Colburn.*

Decorative pillow made from obi fabric by June Colburn. *Photo courtesy of designer.*

This maru obi from the early Taisho period has leaves with mon designs, giving it a strong graphic presence. $150-200

Hand painted on black satin silk, this Nagoya obi shows the Ship of Seven Treasures, a reference to the good fortune gathered by trading. $80-120

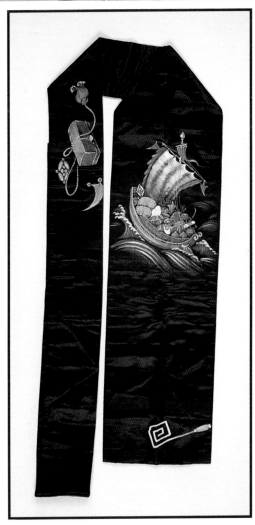

Maru obi with sumi-e painting of duck in grasses. Probably from the 1910 to 1920s era, it would have been worn for informal visiting occasions. $40-70

Two sides of one fukuro obi make it a more useful accessory. Hand painted bamboo over thin stripes, with a reverse side of yellow satin having a stenciled design of clover. This may have been worn by a geisha. Taisho,1910 to 1920s. $100-200

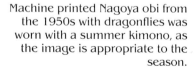

Machine printed Nagoya obi from the 1950s with dragonflies was worn with a summer kimono, as the image is appropriate to the season.

An origami design of a crane decorates the black Nagoya obi from the 1930s. The middle obi is a single width stiff silk called *nishijin*, and is woven with a design of metallic threads of clouds and fringe at the hem, also from the 1930s. White *ro* silk is a summer obi with hand painted red bamboo from the 1950s.

In front are two examples of obi age, the purple one having all over shibori, and the pink with clouds of red that have been created by capping and dyeing. *Obi age from the collection of Shizumi Shigeto Manale*. Obi and obi age $90-200

Pair of *heko-obi* or *kaku obi*, long silk or rayon sashes used to secure men's yukata or kimono. They usually have shibori designs at the edges. Prices vary based on condition. Synthetic $20-50, or silk $50-200

Nagoya obi with red shibori design of blossom on white rinzu silk. Late Showa period. $100-120

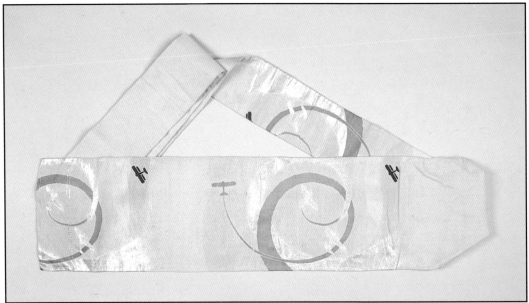

Opposite page:
This is the *oridashi sen*, end of the woven section of an obi.

The vapor trails of airplanes were the inspiration for this obi design. Lightweight silk. Probably mid-1930s. $60-90

A fukuro obi, which is formal, contrasts here with a *sakiori*, rag weave, obi in similar colors. The fukuro also has supplementary weft lacquered threads of dark red. 1960s. $300-400

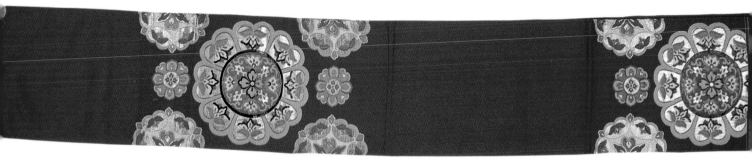

Fukuro obi with flower medallion design. $200-400

Although it appears that three obi are presented here, there are actually two. The outer, narrow obi shows its two sides. This is called a *chuya* obi, for the contrast of dark and light, or day and night. Taisho period. The obi in the center is Nagoya style with a design of ceremonial drum. Early Showa period. $90-300 each

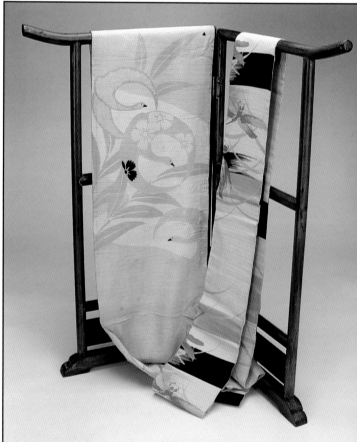

One Nagoya obi with two contrasting sides. Ro silk is used for both, indicating a summer obi, and there is silver thread embroidery detailing on the dragonflies and remnants of couched threads on the cranes; the metallic covering is gone. Probably Taisho.

Young woman's two-sided obi. Early Taisho. $80-120

A *harawase* obi, worn for occasions that are not formal, and having two distinctive fabrics. Early Taisho. $60-90

Three Taisho era obi of ro silk with yuzen designs as well as embroidery detailing. Note the reverse side of contrasting fabrics, which added versatility to the obi as it would be worn for a variety of occasions. Condition varies, with spotting and wear apparent. $50-90

Detail of design.

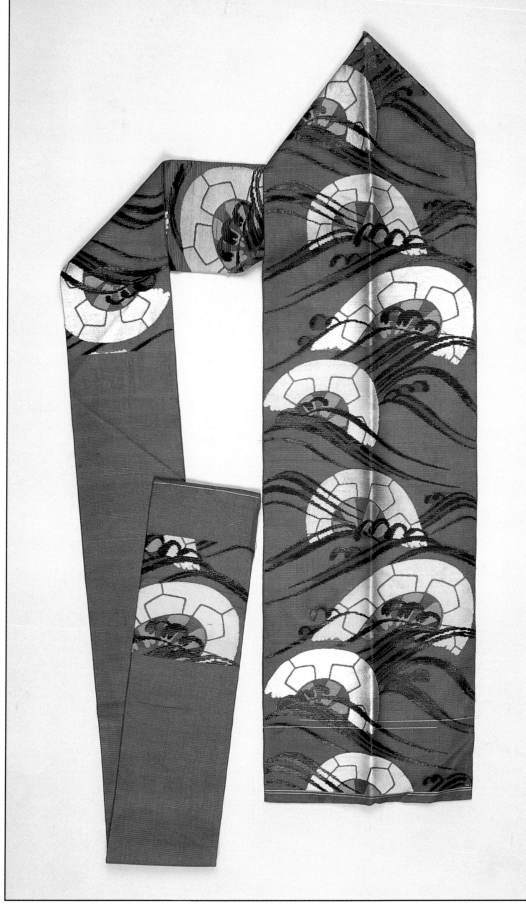

A summer weight, blue Nagoya obi with the black wave of the design in lacquered threads. Late Showa period. $70-100

The gap between the scattered dragon medallions indicates that the obi would be tied in such a way that the blank area would be concealed. 1940 to 1950s. $150-200

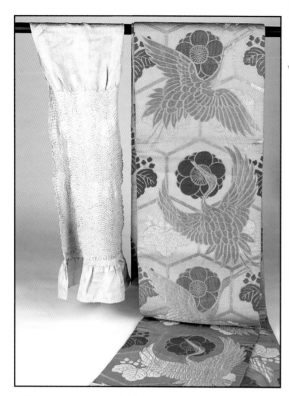

A fragment of an obi with brocade lion design.

These pieces could be worn or displayed together: a wide fukuro obi in shades of pale blue and gold metallic thread, that is suitable for a wedding kimono, and an obi age of blue and white shibori underneath. Late Showa period, 1970s. Obi, $400-600. Obi age about $100-200

The orange obi is fukuro and patterned only on one side. Showa,1970s. The narrow one is deep purple with gold thread design among the orange bamboo leaves. Showa, 1950s. $250-350 each

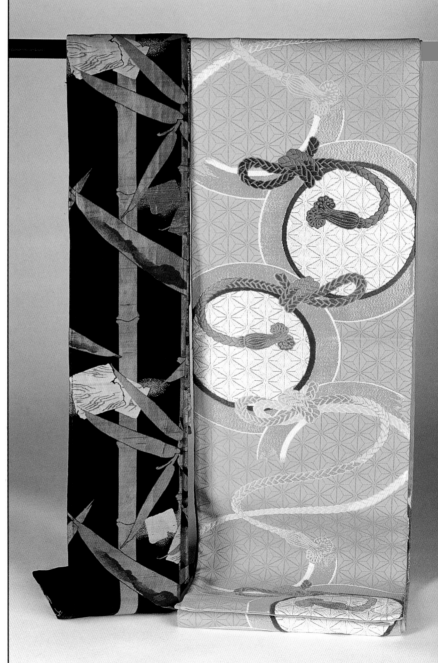

Two obi from the Showa period: an un-sewn roll of obi fabric, in a *sha* weave, a sheer weight suitable for summer and featuring a water design; and a *sentsu* maru obi with stylized flower and butterfly pattern along the full length of one side only. This green obi is suitable for wear with a furisode, a coming-of-age kimono, or for display on its own. A 1930s, Taisho period Nagoya obi with shibori pine lozenge pattern and metallic gold and silver thread embroidery detailing. The wheel is a Buddhist symbol for never-ending existence. $300-600

Two maru obi in shades of royal purple. The overall design of ferns in gold indicates a ceremonial or performance obi, while the other is more of a visiting obi with its design of flowering thistles; it is a fukuro obi. $250-450 each

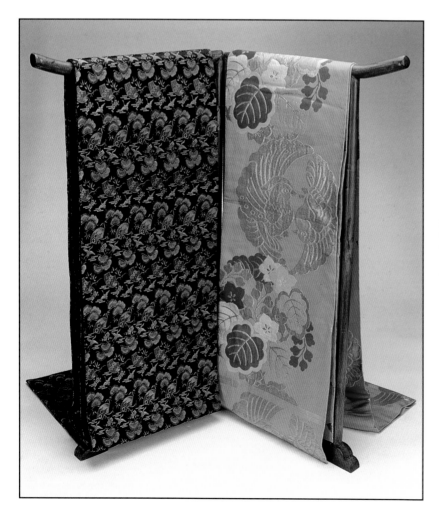

Pair of maru obi. The orange one has symbols adapted from Chinese influence with the pair of birds in opposition and the group of paulownia and cherry blossoms. The brown and gold obi has a tiny design of cranes and is probably from the Taisho period, 1920 to 1930s. $300-500 each

Group of three wide obi with cranes for long life and other traditional symbols for happiness and wisdom. The black one is a fukuro, with design on over half the length of one side and solid black on the other. The red one has a single symbol of a crane for a thousand years of life. Mid-Showa period. Good condition. $250-500

Black ro silk with bamboo design of metallic silver threads and earthen colored wheel. Fukuro style. Mid-Showa period. $150-250

Group of three obi in shades of orange. Two maru, the wide one on the rack and the one folded in front, have metallic threads highlighting the designs for flowers and birds. The third, a narrower width, has elegant weave and the colors are rich. $300-600 each

Both obi are *hon-bukuro*, woven as a tube. The beige one is slightly longer and may be an *odori* obi used in ceremonies. It has images of scrolls which may link it to education. The dark green and gold one has a winter feeling to it, and both are probably late Taisho period. $300-400 each

A pillow made from an obi and a ceremonial pillow cover, *zabuton*, flecked with gold surihaku.

Three *nishijin* obi with the gold bar at the ends which is called the *oridashi sen*, the edge of the woven area. When tied for a kimono, this area will not show. All of these obi feature strong images of birds and symbolic settings. The middle one is Taisho, and the others are Showa period. $400-700

Mid-Meiji period black rinzu kimono with five mon that are executed in large stitches and may have been made for export. It is flanked by two maru brocade obi in deep gold tones with cranes and pines. Kimono $800-900. Obi $400-450

Detail of crane on obi.

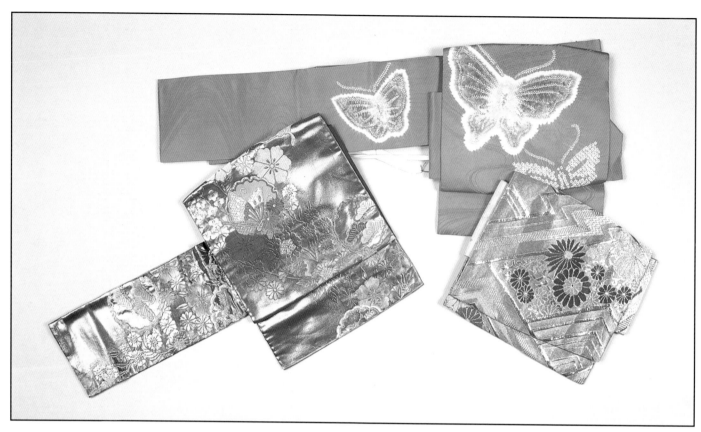

Three *tsuke* obi pre-tied for putting on easily and quickly. They are tied in the *taiko*, the drum bow knot. Late 1970s. $60-90 each

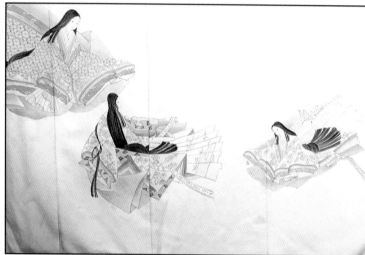

Images from a kimono design.

Accessories used with kimono.

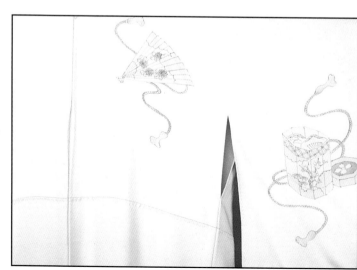

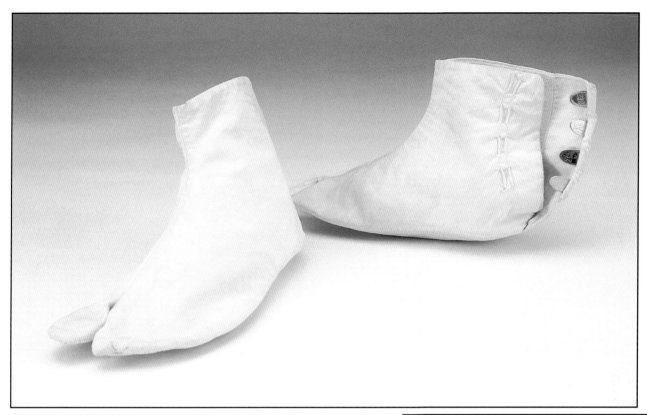

Traditional white cotton tabi socks with metal tabs for securing them around the ankle. $20-30

Essentials for kimono wear: lacquered *getta*, platform shoes; a *date eri* collar cover; and stretch tabi socks.

Purse and *zori*, sandals worn formally. The purse is western style, but the pattern is a traditional tortoiseshell in orange and silver. Late 1980s. $30-50 each

Kame ka zori, hair ornaments made of silk. $40-75

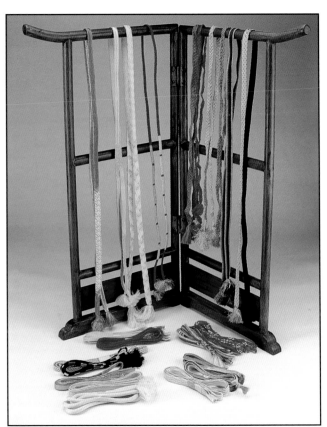

A variety of *obi-jime*, the braided silken cord that secures the obi. It is tied over the obi at the front, and the tasseled ends are tucked around back. $20-30 each

Examples of shibori. On the rack are linings and below are obi age, soft sashes used to decorate as well as secure the kimono. The obi age, with elaborate shibori dyeing, peeks out at the top of the obi like a fancy trim.

Sukiya-bukuro, small carrying cases that represent traditions begun in Edo times, contain small implements carried by a bride tucked into her obi. They include a symbolic knife, to show her willingness to defend her family's honor at all times, and a mirror for checking one's appearance. 1960s. $25-45

Miyabi, is a small rectangular bamboo basket bottom with a silk upper of hand-painted wisteria blossoms. *Sukiya-bukuro* is a small brocade bag for a few tiny things. These could have been made for a child's kimono set. $50-100 each

Leather case with a carved container, possibly made of ivory, called an *inro*. The top screws off and perhaps a fragrance was put in or a lightening bug to guide one's footsteps at night. A mirror and small pocket are found within the case and a mountain scene is on the back. $80-150

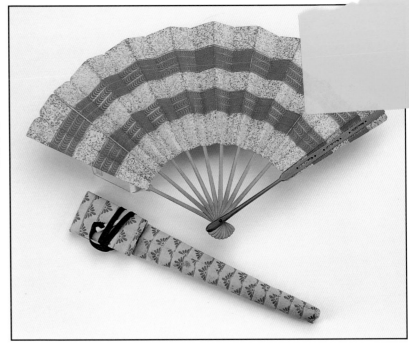

This type of fan is called an *oh-gi*. It is used during the practice of dances. This antique fan is made of paper with carved bamboo ends and a silk brocade case is used for its storage. Early Showa period. $150-200

Two fans with calligraphy and one with people playing wrestling games. *Ki me gai yo* - the lyrics to the national song, are printed on the middle one. An emperor god is on the right, and a game to play an instrument is on the left.

Group of three fans showing that most fans have a pleasing decoration on the reverse side as well as the front. Fans were worn by both men and women tucked into the obi. People replace their fans every year, and may offer them as tribute at their place of worship.

Folk art circular fans with shibori design, made in the Chinese style in Japan, are displayed on both sides of an indigo drawstring purse with decorative *sashiko* stitching. All items are new.

Antique fans called *uchi-wa* were made of paper. Chinese in origin, the red and green combination is more of a Chinese than a Japanese aesthetic. $20-50, depending on condition

7. Women's Haori ~ Short Silk Jackets

Although in Japan the *haori* (ha-or-ee) fell out of favor in the 1970s, these short silk jackets have proved popular with Western women as an item to be worn instead of a blazer. They are not meant to close, but are made to be worn open. The meaning in Japanese is "Folded Wing". Men originally wore them, but geisha popularized them in the Edo period. A haori is worn to keep the kimono from getting soiled, and therefore haori sleeves are susceptible to spotting and stains.

Haori seams are blind stitched, so if you find the lining attractive, turn it inside out and wear it that way. The lower part of haori sleeves can be used as external pockets - reach into the opposite one for ease of access. Some haori have ties called *kumihimo* that are tied in a flat knot, or not at all.

Formal haori have the family mon at the back, either stitched or hand painted.

Sleeve of haori with stencil design

View of a lining showing the kumihimo tie left on.

A fudangi, probably worn as an outer jacket to go to work. Chirimen silk with Taisho style flowers done by yuzen. Lining is tattered shibori of thin silk. Gold cord kumihimo. *Good Goods Collection.*

Group of three homongi haori for visiting with metallic thread accents. Fair condition. Late Showa period. $60-85

The haori on the left is light wool with tiny circles for a conservative design. On the right, the lively yellow resembles a flower-filled garden. For a young woman, both are likely machine silk screened. Late Showa, 1960s. $50-90 each

Red and white shibori with longish sleeves in pristine condition. Lined in pink and white silk with kumihimo, ties on the inside, in red and silver. Mid-Showa period.

The haori on the left is probably late Taisho period with a gray background, tiny cluster of three dots, and stylized cherry blossom design that emerges from a small flower to a hexagonal design. Partially lined with orange printed fabric, it has good kumihimo of pale blue and pink. The haori on the right has a wood-grain design background with medallions of flowers. Mid-Showa period. $70-90 each

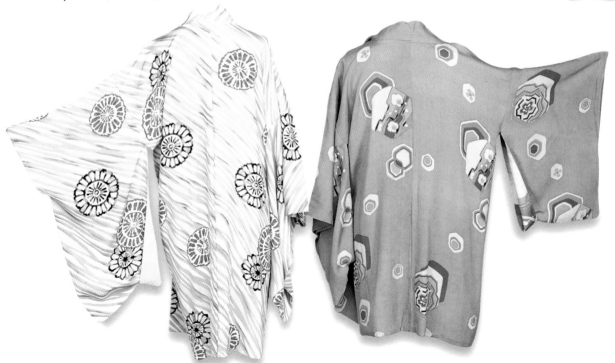

Haori made of Okinawan style cloth called *bingata*. The designs are produced by stenciling and the silk is crepe-like but lightweight. 1970s. $60-90 each

Three haori with different techniques: the gray one has a subdued rinzu of small ovals and its only decoration is the openwork kumihimo edged in gold, which are revealed when the lapels are turned back, 1960s. The middle one is meisen ikat, knee length, and probably from the 1950s. Its design of thistles is very unusual. The last one is probably a silkscreen print in the style of Okinawan stencil printing. It seems abstract, but look closely and see a thatched house in the mountains. 1960s. $60-120 each

Group of three graceful haori in pastel grays and blues. 1960s. $60-150 each

The outer two haori are subtlely dip-dyed and all three have metallic thread machine decoration. Late Showa period. $100-200 each

The haori with green kumihimo ties is probably the oldest of this group, from the early Showa period. It has a dark background with red accents and some silver thread work. The maroon one is very good silk that has a printed design of *go sho* dolls. In the middle, the bold leaf design is also printed and has a lining of white rinzu with ovals and good kumihimo. $80-200 each

Group of three plum-colored haori that have used stencils to produce the designs. 1960s. $60-120 each

Group of three haori in blue, each with white lining and kumihimo. Late Showa period. $60-120

Ikat haori, taken up at the waist, possibly to make it fit a smaller person. Vivid lining. Mid-Showa period. $60-80

Morning mist rises from the mountains in this hand-painted haori done in sumi-e style with indigo inks.

The roses of a sunset, possibly a companion piece to the morning haori. 1960s. It is possible that the colors used to paint the silk were extracted from eggplant or *shizo*, a Japanese herb that is used to color pickled plums. $60-75

Unusual lobster lining, probably from the late 1960s.

Orange rinzu of tiny pine bushes with medallions of phoenix birds facing each other. This is a motif adapted from the Chinese. The lining, however, is quite something else. $150-200

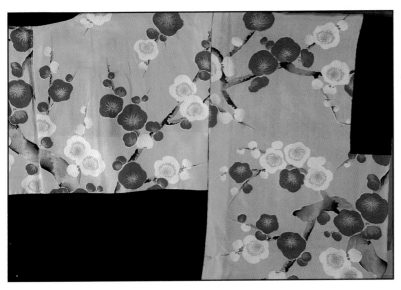

Linings can be very different from the exterior; here a plain black exterior reveals a spirited motif on the lining.

Peach rinzu silk homongi haori with cloud, water, and flower design probably has had a rice paste resist technique used to produce the rose design on the back and front left sleeve. Kumihimo is of carved coral beads. Showa, 1950 to 1960s. $140-180

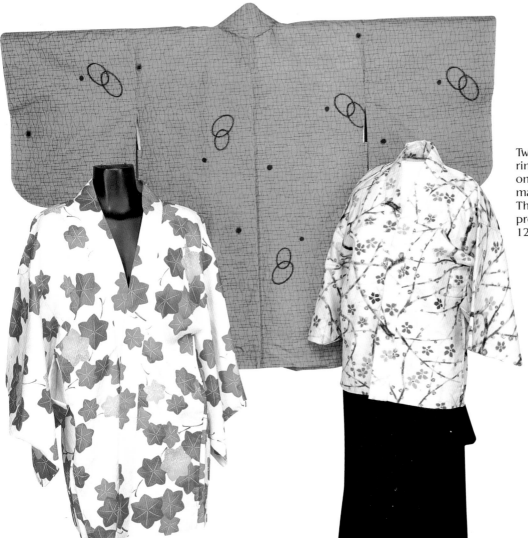

Two ikat and one print over rinzu haori. The very short one on the mannequin has a manufacturer's stamp inside. The coral and black one is probably from the 1930s. $60-120 each

Stencil dyeing and ikat are surface design techniques used in this group. $60-100 each

Group of three haori, one being a lightly padded jacket of woven ikat resembling chess pieces. The middle one has a wood grain ikat pattern. On the left is one with a stencil design of flowers. $80-100

A stenciled ikat of flowers with supplementary weft accents in white and a dip-dyed lining of orange and turquoise on white with surihaku. Good kumihimo. 1930s. $120-160

Different techniques are popular at different times, and these pieces were most likely made during the Taisho period, 1912-1926. This group of three shibori dyed haori are in purple tones. *Good Goods Collection.*

Meisen ikat haori with bold stripes. Wide beige strips seem to have been woven on top of four flower surface designs. 1930s. $100-150

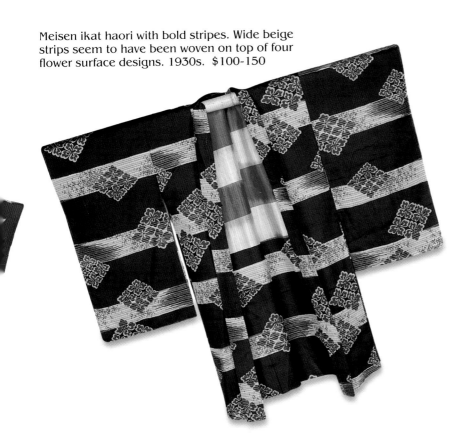

Detail of a shibori design with hand-painted flowers inside the resisted white area.

Early Taisho period weft ikat of trees and mountains in the background with the quality of a watercolor. $90-120

Do chu gi, a large jacket that ties on the inner right and outer left sides and was worn over a fudangi kimono by a woman going to work. It provides another layer to keep her warm in the winter. In the style of the late 1950s. $120-150

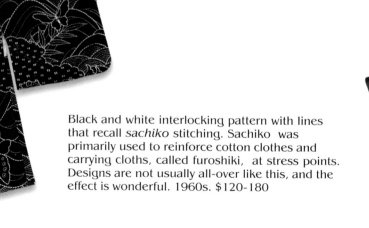

Black and white interlocking pattern with lines that recall *sachiko* stitching. Sachiko was primarily used to reinforce cotton clothes and carrying cloths, called furoshiki, at stress points. Designs are not usually all-over like this, and the effect is wonderful. 1960s. $120-180

From left to right: hand painted design of bamboo leaves lined in white rinzu silk; black and white stencil of water and flowers; and black with rinzu design of florals with a white design of contrasting vertical and diagonal stripes in white. Showa period, 1960s. $80-120 each

Group of decorated black haori of high quality silk with yuzen technique painting and same color embroidery detailing. 1960s to early 1970s. $120-200 each

Sheer black haori in a weave called sha with silvery underside accented with delicate plants and beautifully handwoven kumihimo in pink and white. 1950-1960s. $80-120

Sheer ro silk women's haori with one finely embroidered crest on the back at the center. $70-100

Stunning pair of haori utilizing coloration of rust, gold and silver. Large chrysanthemums cover the one on the left and wavy fans with chrysanthemums over a rinzu silk on the right. Late Showa period. $180-240 each

High quality, heavyweight silk haori decorated with a scene of a pastoral Japanese countryside done in metallic threads. It has white rinzu lining with a white kumihimo. $100-150

Detail of scene.

Landscape detail from a haori used for formal visiting occasions.

Elegant yuzen design of fall flowers graces the back and front left side and sleeve of this haori. Edges of flowers are enhanced with surihaku. The lining is white with a beige print of flowers, and there is an interesting kumihimo of colored leather with a bead in the center. Late Showa period. $250-300

Dramatic blocks of rust, gold, and silver supplementary weft design cover a rinzu of small squares and good clear mon. Excellent condition. Late Showa period. $160-200

Beautiful design of blue, gold, and silver metallic threads with one mon resisted at the center of the back. Heavy silk. *Good Goods Collection.*

Do chu gi, a large jacket that ties on the inner right and outer left sides, with metallic threads woven into water patterns and a velvet collar. Made of wool or synthetic material, it is lined in cotton. Excellent condition. 1950s. $150-180

8. Michiyuki ~ Overcoats

Michiyuki (me-chee-you-kee) are double-breasted, square-necked garments worn, much as a western overcoat, when going outside. The unusual features of michiyuki are their covered snaps and a front pocket at the waist. Sometimes the neckline is a deep "V", depending on the style or preference of the wearer. Today, michiyuki can be worn as a dress, turned around with the buttons in the back, tied at the hip, and accessorized with a necklace.

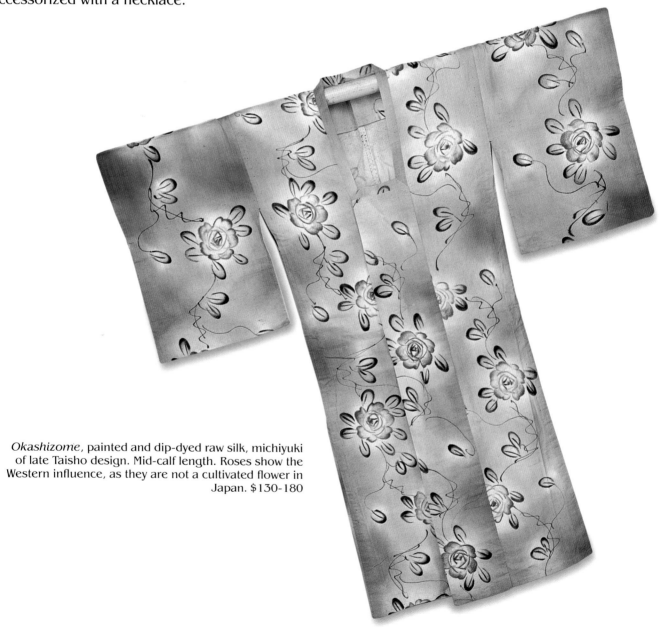

Okashizome, painted and dip-dyed raw silk, michiyuki of late Taisho design. Mid-calf length. Roses show the Western influence, as they are not a cultivated flower in Japan. $130-180

Genrokusode refers to the rounded sleeve of this short and sweet michiyuki which has a deep rose under tone with supplementary weft lacquered thread work all over in reds, golds, and silver. 1920 to 1930s. $80-120

Child's michiyuki-like garment, most likely a coat. Frog closures are adapted from Chinese garments. Meisen woven ikat warp and weft. Taisho period, 1920s. $125-150

Possibly a child's michiyuki, or at least of a design that was popular in the early part of the century. Blue rinzu silk with two white frogs for a closure. $150-180

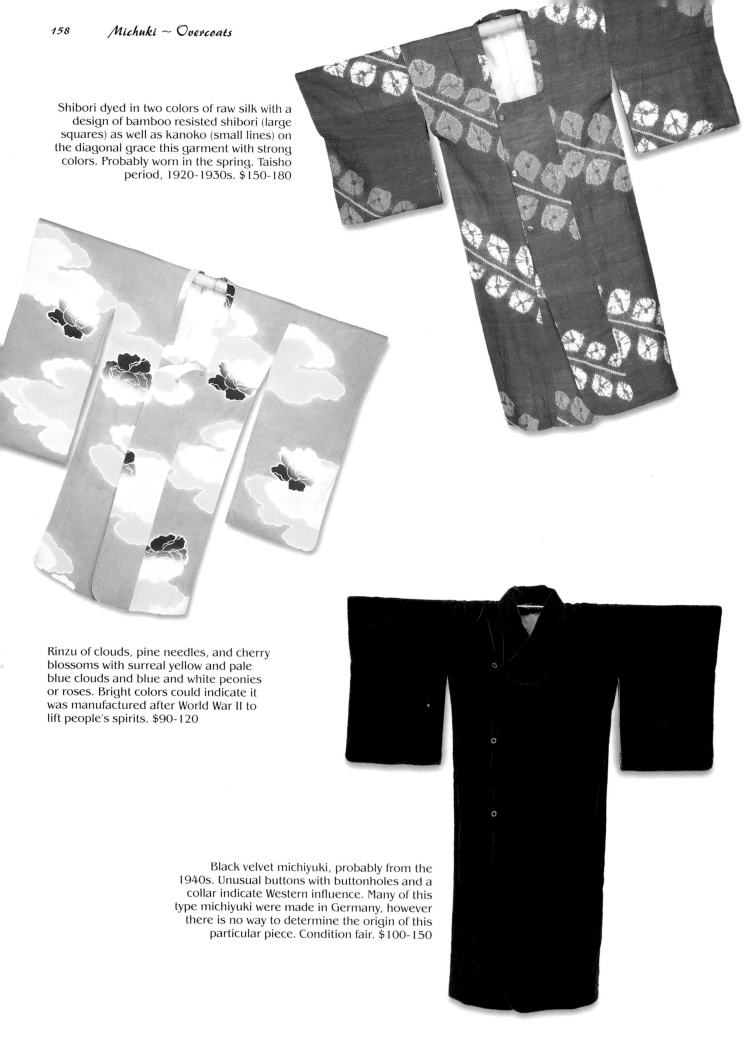

Shibori dyed in two colors of raw silk with a design of bamboo resisted shibori (large squares) as well as kanoko (small lines) on the diagonal grace this garment with strong colors. Probably worn in the spring. Taisho period, 1920-1930s. $150-180

Rinzu of clouds, pine needles, and cherry blossoms with surreal yellow and pale blue clouds and blue and white peonies or roses. Bright colors could indicate it was manufactured after World War II to lift people's spirits. $90-120

Black velvet michiyuki, probably from the 1940s. Unusual buttons with buttonholes and a collar indicate Western influence. Many of this type michiyuki were made in Germany, however there is no way to determine the origin of this particular piece. Condition fair. $100-150

Unlined rust colored garment with woven weft of swallows and a bridge. The threads of this part of the design are visible on the backside with the willows in the background, though their threads do not show on the back. 1950s. $120-180

Many michiyuki have square necks, though occasionally they have with a graceful scalloped neckline. Rinzu silk of geometric design with large floral that is made to look like lacquer. Note the bright floral lining. Early Showa period.

Satin sheen of bamboo design in unusual colors, red and black. Large and long, this michiyuki was probably used in the late 1980s when michiyuki were at the end of their popularity. $60-90

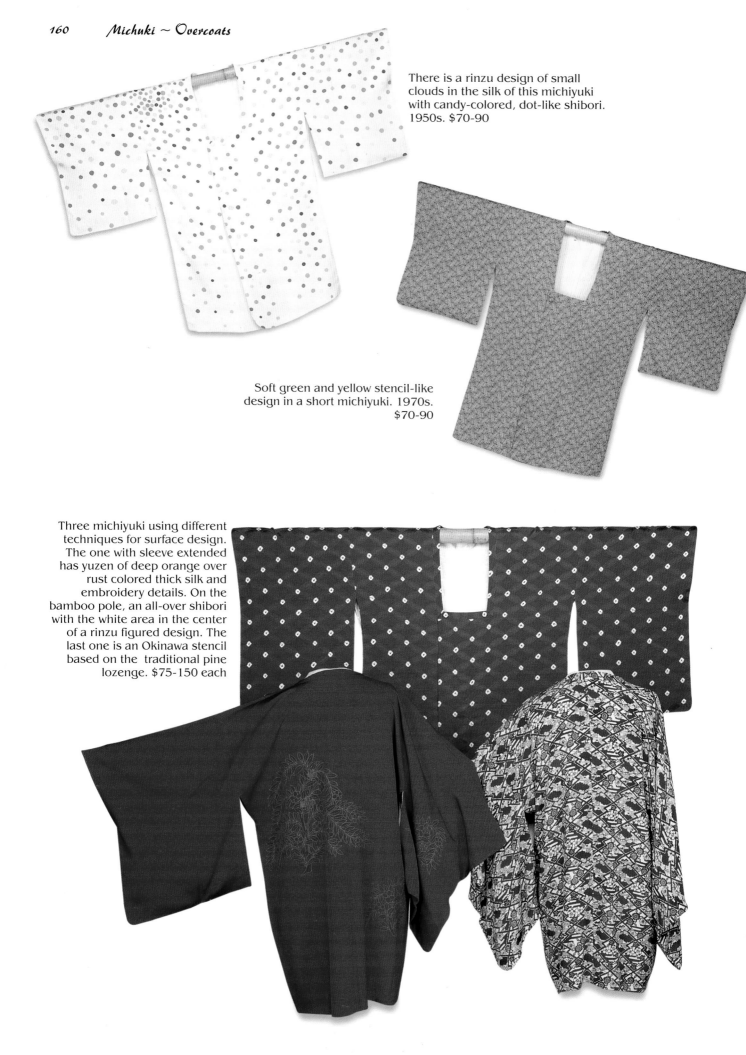

There is a rinzu design of small clouds in the silk of this michiyuki with candy-colored, dot-like shibori. 1950s. $70-90

Soft green and yellow stencil-like design in a short michiyuki. 1970s. $70-90

Three michiyuki using different techniques for surface design. The one with sleeve extended has yuzen of deep orange over rust colored thick silk and embroidery details. On the bamboo pole, an all-over shibori with the white area in the center of a rinzu figured design. The last one is an Okinawa stencil based on the traditional pine lozenge. $75-150 each

These michiyuki make a nice group of reds and purples, suitable for fall and winter wear. The sleeves are turned outward to show the linings. $80-150 each

During a short period, possibly in the late 1930s, there appeared michiyuki made of velvet or combined with velvet. Some had "Made in Germany" labels. $80-200

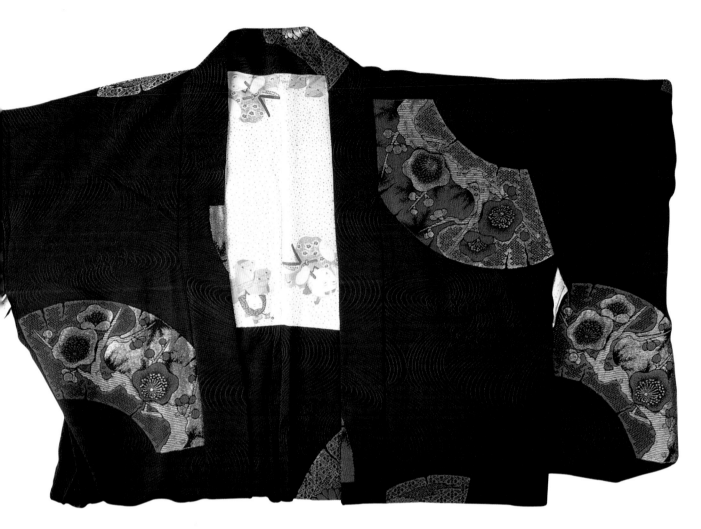

The lining of this decorated black haori has material that could be used for a small child's garment. $60-75

A pony? Cowhide? Who was the person who wore this and why? Good quality fake fur. It has to be from the 1960s. $100-120

9. Men's Apparel

Japanese men's clothing is very conservative, with brown, black and gray the normal colors. Men's individual expression is found in the *nagajuban* (undergarment), which is seen only at home, and in the haori's lining. As the haori is a sort of overcoat, the lining is glimpsed when the garment is taken off. Then the wearer may show motifs that indicate his particular interests: a love of poetry, theater, the mountains where he was born, etc. In the West, women as well as men often find these jackets appealing.

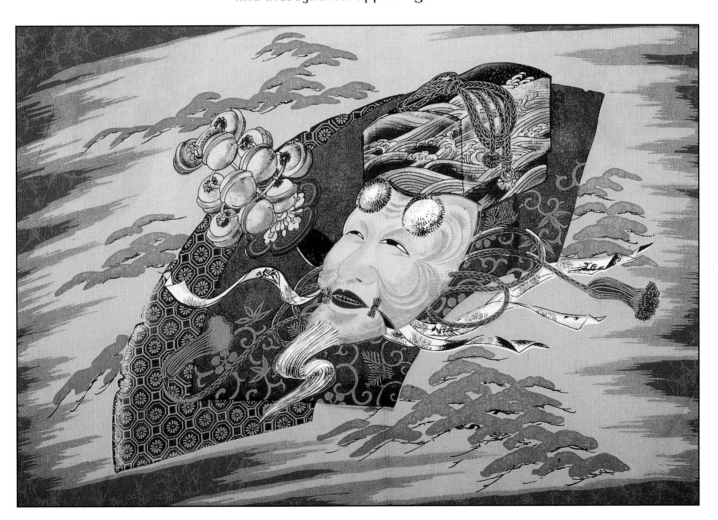

Motif from a man's nagajuban

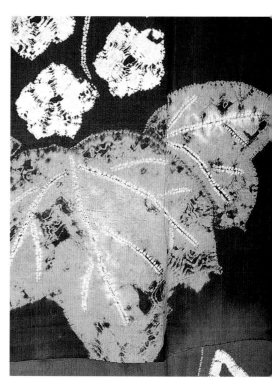

Detail of leaf.

This kimono is a mystery. Perhaps it is not complete. It is a man's style with rough black silk outer fabric and a lining on the sleeves and entire back of shibori resist and dip-dyeing. *Good Goods Collection*

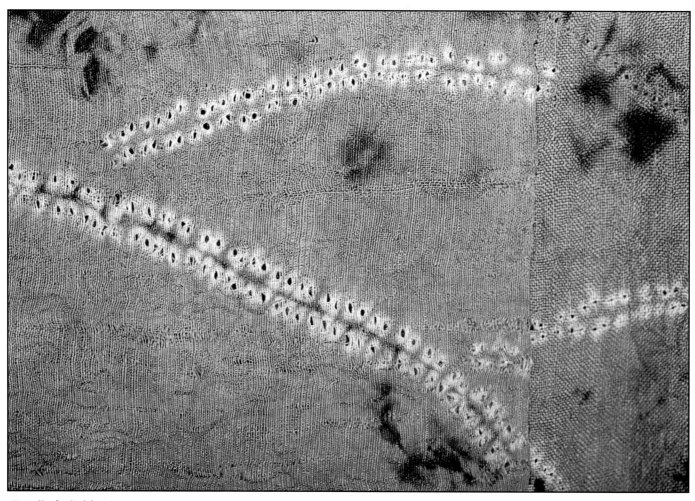

Detail of stitching.

These dolls represent male figures that are part of three different Girl's Day sets. They are missing their instruments and wear costumes of the Imperial court of the Heian period, 794-1192. $25-100 each.

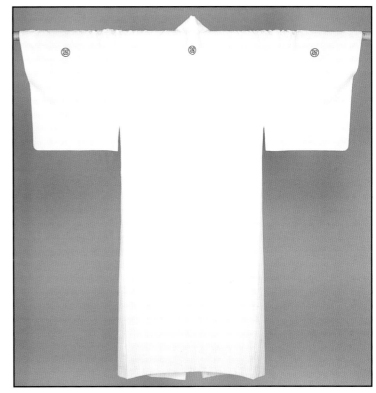

White kimono with five crests of gold mon, indicating the highest level of formal dressing. This would be worn under a hakama during a ceremony. $150-250

The placement of three family crests on a formal kimono.

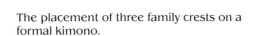

Crossed hawk feathers is the mon worn by families with the name Takaha.

A folded fan, *ao gi*, and pine needles, *matsu*, form this family crest.

A mon of paper mulberry, *kaji*.

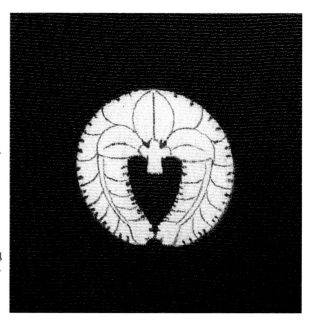

The symbol representing the wisteria, *fuji*.

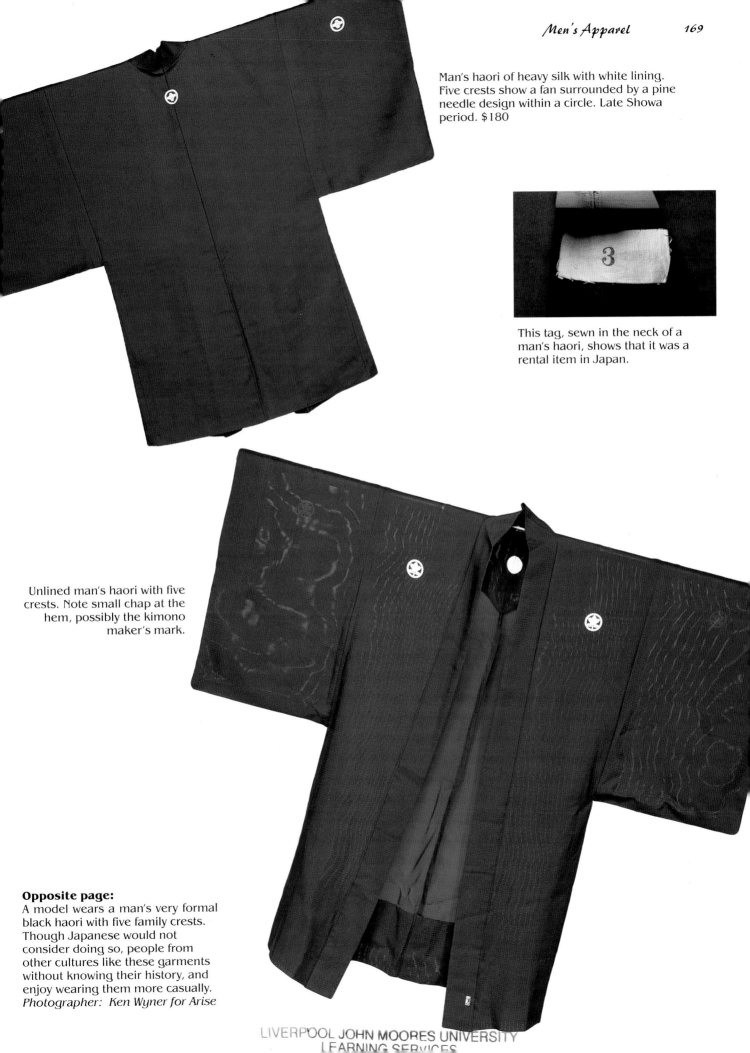

Man's haori of heavy silk with white lining. Five crests show a fan surrounded by a pine needle design within a circle. Late Showa period. $180

This tag, sewn in the neck of a man's haori, shows that it was a rental item in Japan.

Unlined man's haori with five crests. Note small chap at the hem, possibly the kimono maker's mark.

Opposite page:
A model wears a man's very formal black haori with five family crests. Though Japanese would not consider doing so, people from other cultures like these garments without knowing their history, and enjoy wearing them more casually.
Photographer: Ken Wyner for Arise

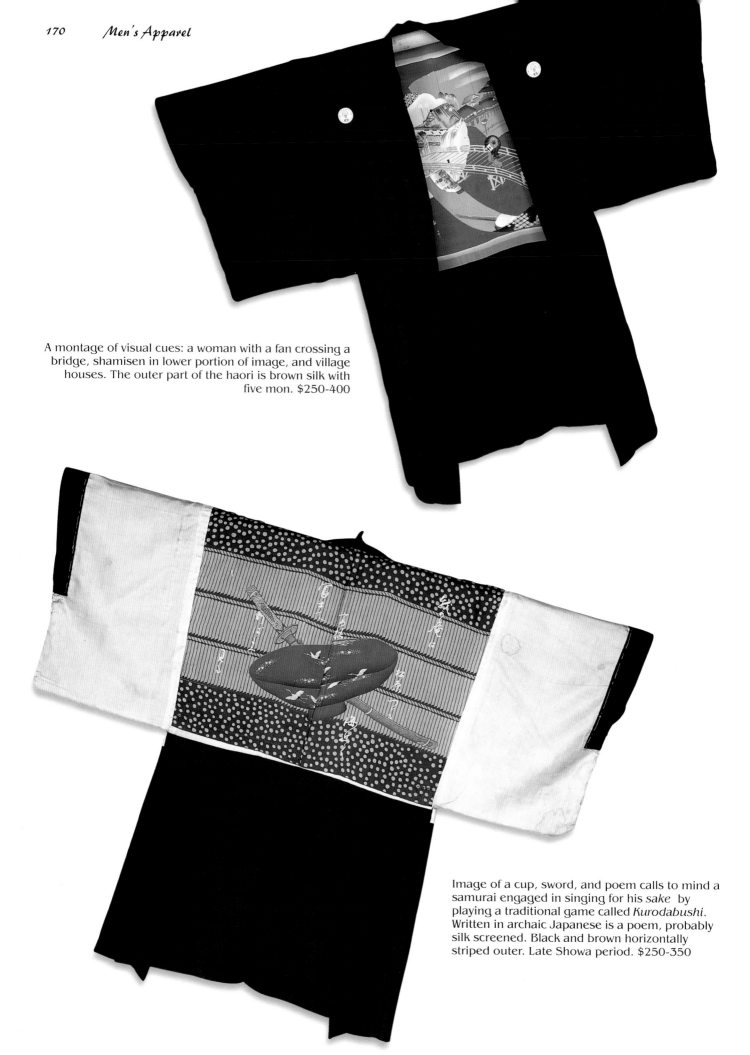

A montage of visual cues: a woman with a fan crossing a bridge, shamisen in lower portion of image, and village houses. The outer part of the haori is brown silk with five mon. $250-400

Image of a cup, sword, and poem calls to mind a samurai engaged in singing for his *sake* by playing a traditional game called *Kurodabushi*. Written in archaic Japanese is a poem, probably silk screened. Black and brown horizontally striped outer. Late Showa period. $250-350

長松生風�(?)
古潤土水修白出
玉府飯(?)梅水景
致動移子仕
老(?)級
哲年(?)

Lining showing a pine tree trunk and branches with a poem about waiting for the New Year's celebration and the happiness it will bring. Probably silk screened, it has an interesting five-crest mon. 1950s. $250-350

Lining with a background of ships and two squares with poetic images of waves and a tiger, probably silkscreened. Black outer with five crests. $275-375

Contemplative brocade lining compressing the distance between the images. Late Showa period. $350-450

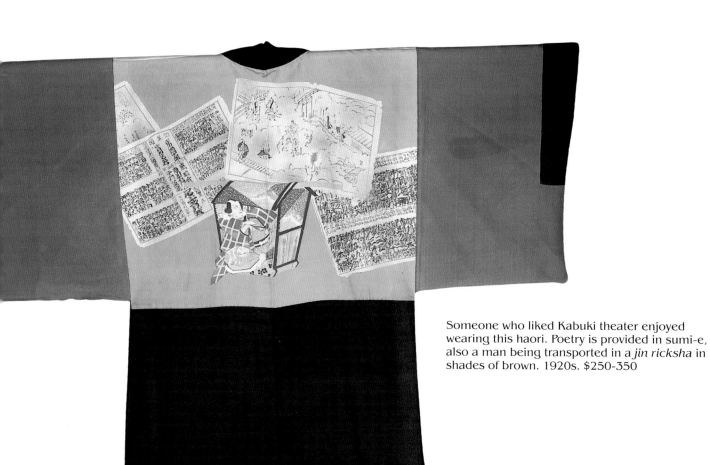

Someone who liked Kabuki theater enjoyed wearing this haori. Poetry is provided in sumi-e, also a man being transported in a *jin ricksha* in shades of brown. 1920s. $250-350

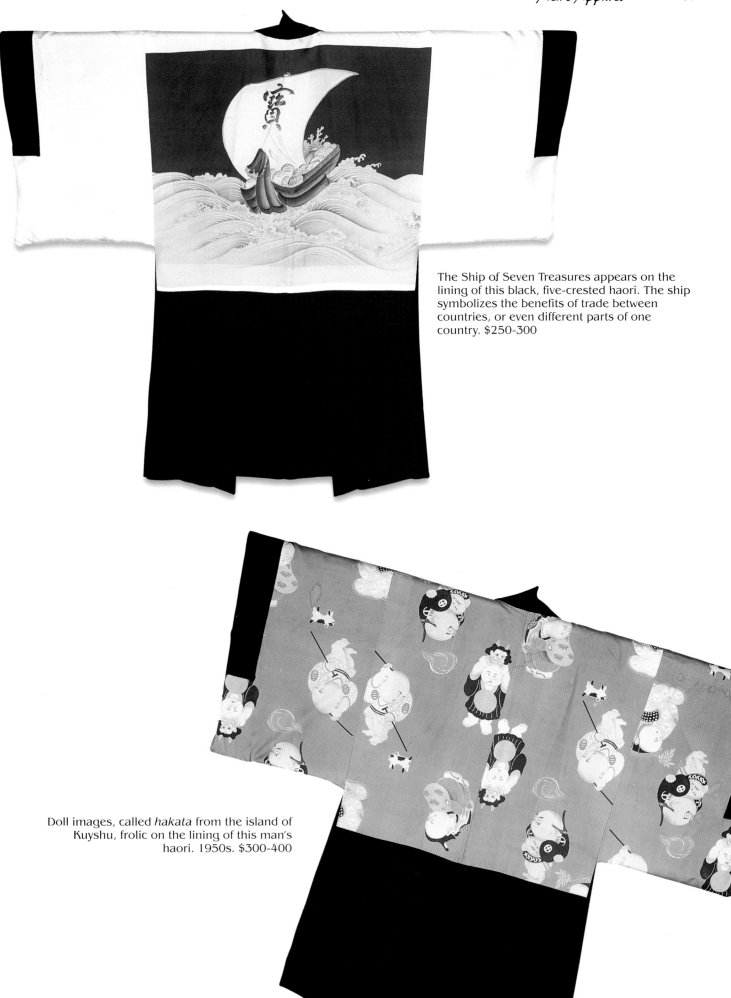

The Ship of Seven Treasures appears on the lining of this black, five-crested haori. The ship symbolizes the benefits of trade between countries, or even different parts of one country. $250-300

Doll images, called *hakata* from the island of Kuyshu, frolic on the lining of this man's haori. 1950s. $300-400

Unusual shibori lettered lining with brown raw silk outer fabric. The poem, about beautiful minds and beautiful clouds, is signed in the lower corner. A stitched mon is on the back. $350-450

This lining has a thatched hut, cormorant bird used in fishing, and a bridge with Mount Kamo in the background. The outer fabric is plain black silk of medium grade. Late Showa period. $250-350

Woven lining of a temple compound with
a mountain the distance. The right side of
the garment is dark brown without a mon.
Late Showa period. $350-450

Lining showing Mt. Fuji and a river with a small rowboat and two
men. The out side is black with five mon. 1960s. $400-450

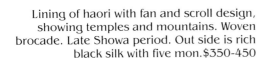

Lining of haori with fan and scroll design, showing temples and mountains. Woven brocade. Late Showa period. Out side is rich black silk with five mon.$350-450

Brown raw silk outer fabric with lining showing the Ship of Seven Treasures moving towards people watching from the land. Archaic Chinese characters, possibly poems, are in the background and poetic Japanese characters are on the ship area. The design is most likely silk screened, with added painted accents. Late 1960s. $200-250

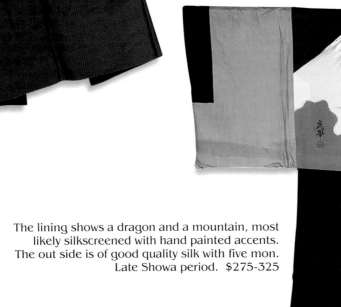

The lining shows a dragon and a mountain, most likely silkscreened with hand painted accents. The out side is of good quality silk with five mon. Late Showa period. $275-325

The lining of a haori has been made into a pillow front by June Colburn.

One way to tame a dragon is to put him under glass. An effective use of the lining from a haori is this framed presentation by June Colburn.

Hakama are worn by men and women as school uniforms, for martial arts, and for other ceremonial occasions. These thin brown and black striped hakama are lightweight silk, probably mid-1960s. $50-70 each.

The hakama with gold background and pine boughs with needles is a heavier silk. Perhaps it was used in a dance performance or a ceremony. 1950 to 1960s. $100-300

10. Uchikake ~ and Other Wedding Kimono

Uchikake (oo-chi-kah-kay) is a type of elaborate kimono with a padded hem that first became popular during the Edo period (1600-1868). The term applies today to a kimono worn by a bride during the traditional part of the wedding ceremony in Japan. It is not secured with an obi but is worn open. Prior to that, brides wore long black kimono, more like a tomesode, for their weddings. The cost of a new uchikake is prohibitively expensive for most families, and they are often rented from a company that specializes in wedding apparel for the entire bridal party. Most of the uchikake shown here date from the 1960s and 1970s. Also included are *furisode* kimono worn by single women below the age of twenty-one.

The crane is frequently seen on wedding textiles, as they represent a wish for long life.

This image of a crane flying high in the mountains over a house may represent an achievement or the mastery of an ability. It is Japanese in construction, but has Tibetan-Chinese coloration and imagery.

Vivid uchikake sleeve from the 1960s with hand embroidery and gold leaf application, called surihaku.

A chuburisode from the early 1960s. White rinzu silk with shibori of limbs and gold embroidery detailing and paulownia flowers as worn at the wedding reception by the bride. *Good Goods Collection*

Detail of the decorative techniques.

Dolls from two separate Girl's Day sets are shown to demonstrate how a uchikake is worn unencumbered by an obi.

Purple is generally reserved for those of royal bearing. This five-
crested kimono has a wonderful design of a peacock who's glorious
feathers are entwined with wisteria flowers and chrysanthemum
leaves. This could mean it was worn in late summer, perhaps as a
costume worn by a dancer. The lining is entirely of red rinzu silk,
which is also not usually seen. Exquisite tiny embroidery details are
placed around the eye, flower centers, and shading of the leaves.
$1500-2000

Possibly from the late Edo or early Meiji period, this blue silk kimono may have been a wedding garment or used in a theater production. Supplementary weft lacquered thread brocade is in two shades. The hem is padded and lined in red silk. Delicate condition. $1200-2000

An unusual set of a kimono with a pleat in the back and a shawl with knotted fringe, they probably were made for export or to mimic some aspects of Western dress. Embroidery of irises is done with relatively thick threads and large stitches, however it is done well. Late 19th to early 20th century. $2000-3000

Opposite page:
Orange-red kimono with all-over hand embroidery work of cranes, chrysanthemums, cherry blossoms, and a couched ribbon-like band connecting them all. 1960s. $750-900

Looking like gold foil, this woven wedding kimono has images of cranes singly and in pairs on the diagonal all over the robe. Lined in red silk. 1960s to 1970s. $800-1000

This kimono tells an interesting story. The building with a culvert, through which passes abundant water, could be a portal to the heavens or enlightenment, as found in the study of Zen Buddhism. The kimono may have been a ceremonial robe, but it strays far from traditional Japanese coloration and execution of image; perhaps it was made in the Japanese style by a person from China. *Good Goods Collection*

Vivid colors and traditional images of cranes, peonies, and waves appear here on crepe silk. Couched detailing is found on the crane's head and wings. $1100-1300

A wedding kimono with a combination of strong and delicate colors. Fans are the prevalent element and there is also a gift cart and wheel. Pale pink and lilac flowers are interwoven, and colorful pine and bamboo is embroidered also. One sleeve needs reattachment. It is lined in red silk. $600-800

An uchikake that combines hand painting, embroidery, and gold couched threads. The peony in the back center is delicately painted by hand, and rich embroidery abounds. Some marks are present from being folded and having the metallic threads leach. Overall, it is in very good condition. 1960s. $1500-1700

Detail.

The white kimono worn under the uchikake is called the *kakeshita*, and would have been tied with an obi. Satin silk is lined in silvery metallic material here. Cranes and pines are hand embroidered, with red accented crests outlined in gold and red is picked up at the hem. The wings have rhinestone outlines. Late 1960s to 1970s. $400-450

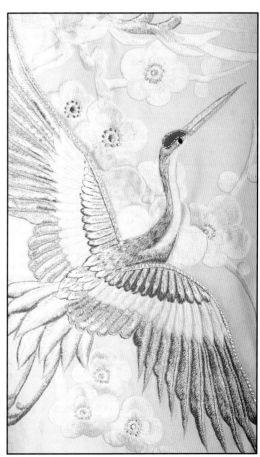

Detail of crane.

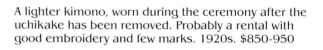

A lighter kimono, worn during the ceremony after the uchikake has been removed. Probably a rental with good embroidery and few marks. 1920s. $850-950

Sleeve detail.

Mid-Showa period, young woman's ... kimono with many interesting patterns within the depiction of a small fishing village: houses, nets, and water all carry parts of other graphic images that tie into the whole. Some embroidery detailing has gold metallic thread. Lined in pale peach silk at the sleeves and hem. 1960-1970. $250-350

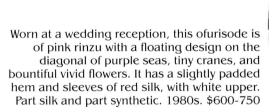

Worn at a wedding reception, this ofurisode is of pink rinzu with a floating design on the diagonal of purple seas, tiny cranes, and bountiful vivid flowers. It has a slightly padded hem and sleeves of red silk, with white upper. Part silk and part synthetic. 1980s. $600-750

Ofurisode of soft pink with gold surihaku accents. A design that falls from the shoulder includes birds, branches, clouds, and waves. 1960s to 1970s. Excellent condition. $420-500

Ofurisode of green over white rinzu with gold surihaku accents; a formal garment with couched thread work. The hem and sleeves are accented with deep red dyeing. Late Showa period, 1960s. Good condition. $550-650

Stunning yuzen design on furisode kimono of chrysanthe- mums and daisies with a large area of couching on the front left; lined with dip-dyed white rinzu silk ending in orange. 1950s to 1960s. $550-650

Lovely chuburisode kimono of white rinzu silk in a wave pattern, with chrysanthemums in an overall design. Yuzen technique on the flowers with gold surihaku accents and gold couching detail on the left front. Lining is spotted by metallic thread, but the outer surface is in very good condition. Showa period, late 1950s. $350-450

Detail of couching on the kimono.

This is a nagagi, a fancy homongi worn in the 1950s to 1960s, with a short sleeve, kosode. It has a white rinzu background with white peonies and lush foliage, gold surihaku, and couching. Sleeves and hem lined in deep orange lightening to white. 1980s. $450-600

11. Children's Kimono

Children have special blessing ceremonies at Shinto and Buddhist temples to which they wear elaborate kimono that are usually made with silk and bear auspicious emblems for happiness and long life. Because of their diminutive size, they can be used effectively in the West for interior decorating accents.

Part of a hem design from a young girl's kimono

This small kimono has been taken in at the shoulders to fit the last wearer. Unusual green and cream color, with a gosho doll image holding Buddhist symbols. Wonderful large mon of waves, it is padded throughout. 1950s. $200-250

A padded boy's kimono with the image of Buddha reading a scroll under a bodhi tree, the tree of wisdom. This baby's kimono is of high quality and in very good condition. Mid-Showa, 1940s to1960s. $150-200

Ikat design of browns and greens in a cotton padded child's kimono lined in pink, probably hand woven. 1920s. $100-120

Two children's kimono in warp and weft ikat Oshima silk. The distinctive brown color is created by mordants in the water where the cloth is woven. The kimono showing the back is in a pine needle design. The one open to show the pink cotton lining has a complex of double tiny crosses and a second shade of brown. Both have been taken in to fit a smaller child than those for which they originally were sewn. Early Showa period. $80-120 each

Child's padded kimono with cranes flying over a sun-like image and a diagonal checkerboard, like a pine bark design, in the background. 1970s. $50-90

Childhood toys and festival images in blue and cream squares. 1950s. $60-90

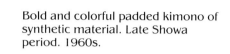

Bold and colorful padded kimono of synthetic material. Late Showa period. 1960s.

Another toy-oriented child's kimono in pale beige and green horizontal wide bands. 1950s. $60-80

Small boy's kimono of silk printed with alternating bands of black and cream with merry samurai. Hand sewn, made in the 1940s. $90-130

Images of toys and travel are on this child's kimono. $100-120

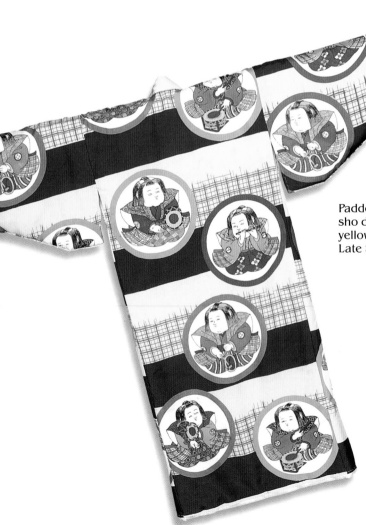

Padded small kimono with images of go sho dolls making music. Alternating yellow and blue horizontal wide bands. Late Showa period. $70-90

Set of two padded pieces with fish, fan,
and samurai helmet. Synthetic material.
Late Showa period. $125-150

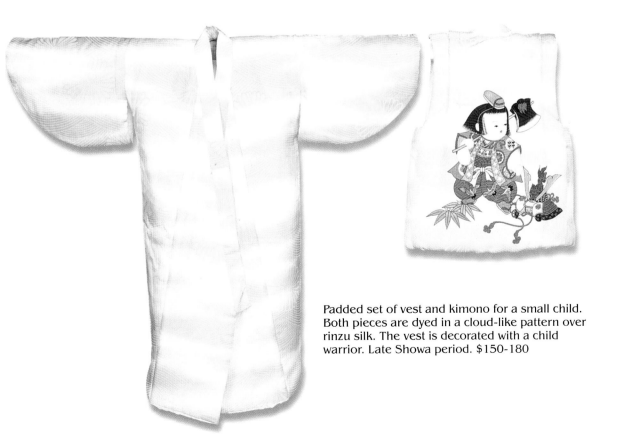

Padded set of vest and kimono for a small child.
Both pieces are dyed in a cloud-like pattern over
rinzu silk. The vest is decorated with a child
warrior. Late Showa period. $150-180

Shi-chi-go-san, worn in November when a child is 7, 5 or 3 years old when they go to a temple for a blessing ceremony. Kimono of silk with various Buddhist symbols painted onto drums and unusual large bamboo mons. 1940s. $120-150

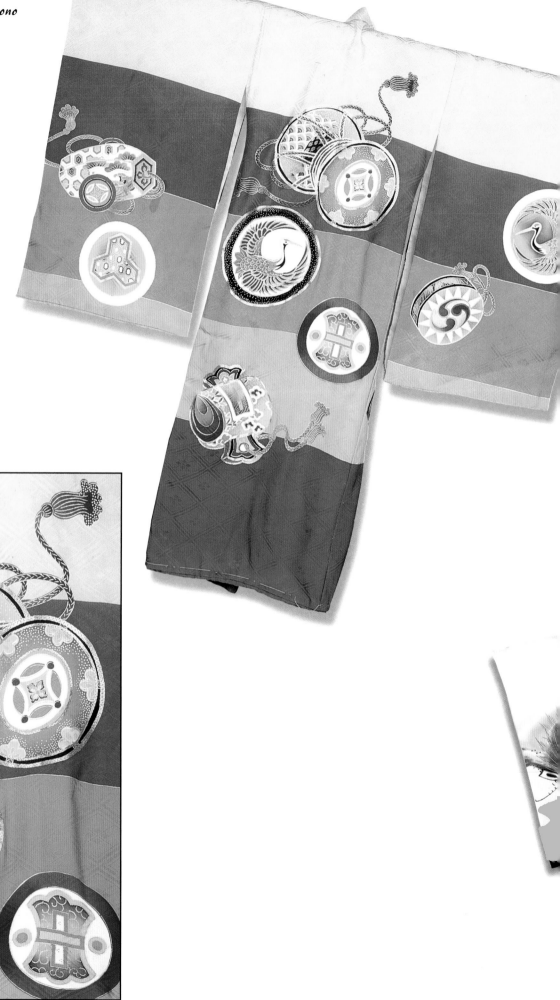

The *Omiyamaidi* is used as part of a Shinto ceremony. The grandmother carries the baby at one month old to a temple for the priest to give the child a blessing. Boy's kimono usually have a black background with the family mon painted in. These two are unusual because of the unpainted mon, possibly it was never worn, and the white color and bold design of the other one. Excellent condition. Recent vintage. $100-200 each

White shibori dots on clouds of green encircle the bold eagle of this rinzu silk kimono. Yuzen design is painted and there are some embroidered accents. Excellent condition. 1930s to 1940s. *Good Goods Collection.*

Rinzu silk and a design of mon emblems are the background for this boy's kimono portraying an eagle landing on a Japanese bridge. Some couched thread work appears. Excellent condition. Late Showa period, 1970s to 1980s. $180-240

Rinzu silk of white that has a dip-dyed hem of rich blue and gold and silver embroidery of dragon and clouds. Possibly made as an export item. Silk, with inner white lining. $500-700

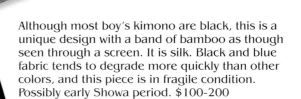

Although most boy's kimono are black, this is a unique design with a band of bamboo as though seen through a screen. It is silk. Black and blue fabric tends to degrade more quickly than other colors, and this piece is in fragile condition. Possibly early Showa period. $100-200

Shichigosan of fish leaping from water. Excellent sumi-e painting. Superior condition. Taisho period. *Collection of Ann Marie Moeller* $300-400

A classic image of Japan with cranes, water, mountains and a castle, with the sun framing the scene. It has sumi-e painting, embroidery details, couched threads, and gold painting surihaku. There is a lot of staining on the front of the sleeves, however, this can be overlooked in terms of the striking image on the back. *Good Goods Collection.*

Padded cotton kimono with crane design and pink ties in front. Fair condition. Late Taisho period. $60-100

A black kimono and a white kimono, each with a pair of cranes. Hand painted with embroidery and couched threads. Mid-Showa period. $150-300, based on condition

Girl's kimono with pink background and red clouds with multi-colored flowers. Taken in at shoulders to fit the last wearer, it is in fair condition. Early Showa period. $40-60

Pink and orange printed girl's kimono, possibly not silk. Excellent condition. $60-90

Orange dyeing suggests water, as it moves from the sleeve to the hem of this girl's garment. It is enhanced with surihaku gold leaf as well as gold and blue embroidery. Mid-Showa period, 1950s to 1970s. $120-150

Detail of delicate and unusual purple butterfly mon at center of back.

Chuburisode, a young girl's kimono in white and bright orange with couched accents. Very good condition. 1970s. $100-140

Opposite page:
Two girl's kimono received from a family collection. An interesting note is that the sleeves are designed to make it look like there are three komono being worn. Actually, there is only the outer layer and a bit of the colorful fabric with a slightly padded white lining pieced in. Embroidery of wisteria appears the front lapels and body, back body, and sleeves, with one delicate family mon stitched in white on the back. Possibly made for a religious ceremony or a parade where the person wearing it represents a princess or some other person of stature. Probably pre-1940. $800-$1200 for pair

Girl's vest of peach silk with yuzen painted patterns. This would make a charming wall hanging. 1940s. $60-90

A unique vest of padded and shibori design on silk with printed material for straps in front. Possibly used to hold a baby. Date unknown. Made from nagajuban material. *Good Goods Collection.*

Yako-san style bast weave fiber set consisting of hakama, a pant-like lower body garment, and a short kimono upper, with extra long sleeves. This may be a dance costume or of ceremonial use. It has a crossed feather mon drawn by hand in a resisted area. Taisho period. $350-450

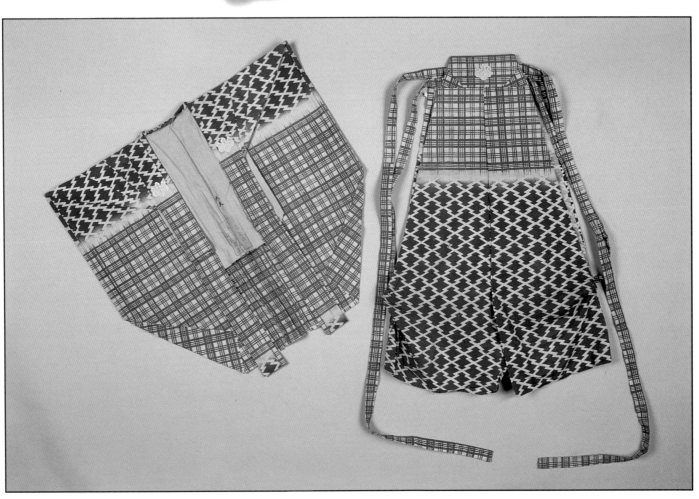

A samurai style, Meiji era outfit consisting of a *kamishimo* upper, designed to broaden the appearance of the shoulders, and a hakama lower. This would have been worn for ceremonial purposes by a child. $200-250

12. Furoshiki and Fukusa ~ Ceremonial Cloths

A *furoshiki* is a square wrapping cloth, used to carry items. It can be simple and made of cotton or more elaborate and made of expensive silk that would be used in combination with a *fukusa*.

The fukusa is a square cloth that is draped over a gift. It is double layered heavier silk, often with gold tassels at the corners and is used as part of the gift-giving process. The front of a fukusa is decorated with auspicious symbols, usually made in a brocade method, but sometimes found hand painted. The family's mon is usually set in gold upon a red field on the reverse side. In the West, their small size makes fukusa a good choice for framing and elegant display.

Reverse side of a fukusa, showing the mon of a paulownia blossom

Yuzen technique creates this image of two cranes framed by a setting sun on chirimen, a heavily textured silk. Reverse is peach colored silk with cherry blossom mon in one corner. Early Taisho. Some soiling. $600-800

Fukusa with crane and turtle, sea and sun background, is a woven design. Corner tassels are knotted to look like a turtle also. Excellent condition. Late Showa period. $300-500

Brocade fukusa of a crane. Clouds are of metallic threads and are of a flatter weave. Turtle tassels at corners; one is missing. 1970s. $200-400

Brown chirimen silk, this furoshiki shows the treasures in front of the Ship of Seven Treasures and two cranes flying nearby - omens of good luck. $500-700

Ship of Seven Treasures motif on large fukusa. Reverse side is red with heavily embroidered gold mon of paulownia leaves. Although only one tassel remains, it is in very good condition. Mid-Showa period. $350-450

A furoshiki with a design that is a combination of printing, hand painting and hand embroidery detailing of the Ship of Seven Treasures. It is made of chirimen silk and backed with red chirimen, and having a paulownia crest resisted in white in one corner. Early Taisho. Excellent condition. $700-900

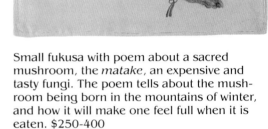

Small fukusa with poem about a sacred mushroom, the *matake*, an expensive and tasty fungi. The poem tells about the mushroom being born in the mountains of winter, and how it will make one feel full when it is eaten. $250-400

Fan with a cherry blossom and pine motif on a machine-woven fukusa. No mon is on the reverse; perhaps this would have been added when it was purchased. Late Showa period. $250-350

On this fukusa, the cranes are entirely hand embroidered and the centers of the pine cones are stitched with gold thread. The sun and pine branches are hand painted. Symbols are for long life. Some wear is on the lower portion where it was folded for storage. 1920s. $400-500

A chirimen furoshiki, used to wrap a present, with an image of *Sanbaso*, a famous ceremonial dancer found in Kabuki, Noh, and New Year's performances. Much used and stained, it nevertheless has an interesting pattern. Early Taisho. $300-500

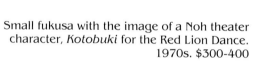

Small fukusa with the image of a Noh theater character, *Kotobuki* for the Red Lion Dance. 1970s. $300-400

Paulownia leaf mon on red ro silk.

Omodaka, water plantain mon.

A crisp mon and even stitching of
white threads accent this red
reverse side of a fusksa.

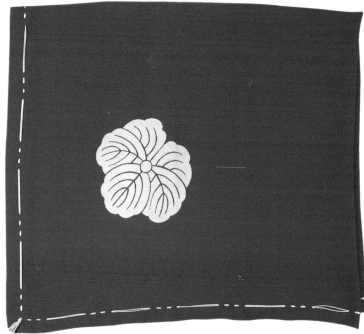

Family crest of *kiri*, paulownia.

This crest comes from a Chinese design and, though it has four distinct areas, it is the seven-treasure shape. In Japanese, it is called *shichiho*.

A child and master play with a toy cannon embroidered with fine stitches of silk floss on good quality white silk background. The reverse is red with a white mon resisted out. Possibly this was given with a gift at the birth of a child. $120-180

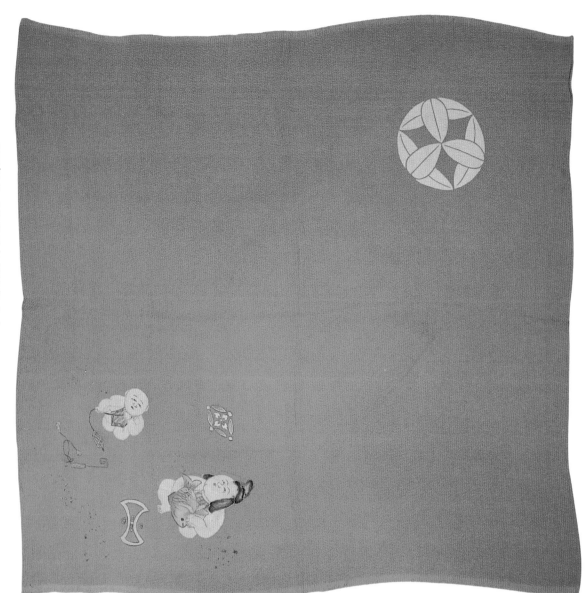

Dip-dyed orange furoshiki with hand drawn corner design of two figures, one with a koi and the other, smaller figure with a small net and double ax. Probably it was used for a Boy's Day gift or for covering a wedding chest. Surihaku gold leaf accent. Early Taisho. One of a pair. $500-700 each.

Okina, the enlightened old man with a long white beard, teaches the next generation. He is a character from the Noh theater tradition. This fukusa features hand embroidery over thickly woven white base. The child with pine bough symbolizes resiliency. A paulownia mon is on the reverse. $120-200

13. Religious and Theater Costumes

Kesa are Japanese Buddhist priest's robes. Fabrics were considered an appropriate gift to give a temple for the compensation of the priests. Sometimes they were made from scraps of discarded or soiled kimono, or the kimono of wealthy women who's husbands had died. Kesa have five, seven or nine panels, alternating short and long, in each one. Kesa is worn draped over the shoulders and is secured with a loop in the front. It is not an easily worn garment, and probably should not be worn, given the sacred nature of its original intent. They are marvelous textiles, and are collectible in the West today.

Generally, Kabuki and No theater costumes are not commonly available for sale, as through use they usually are worn out.

A Shinto priest is wearing a kesa during his New Year's visit to the home of the couple flanking him. Early twentieth century.

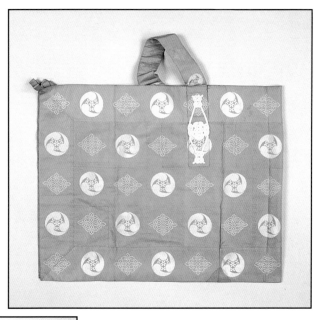

Green silk kesa lined in rust rinzu silk. Mid-Showa period, shown folded. $200-300

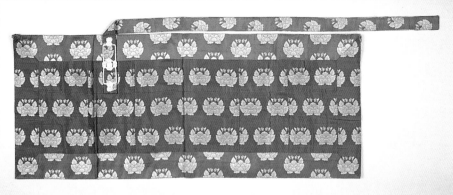

Buddhist garment of heavy gold silk with white cords, shown open. $200-300

Different patterns appear in three sets of Shinto altar pieces. Each set has two pieces, shaped as triangles of different sizes. Silk brocade front with white silk back. Coloration is based on the preference of the family who presents the offering. New. $40-60 each

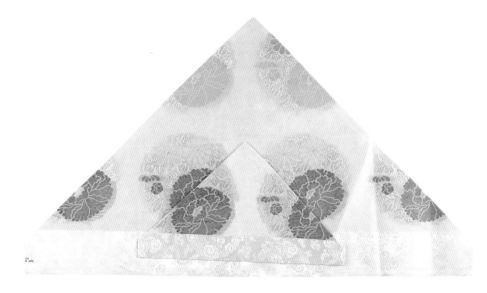

One set of Shinto altar pieces on which ceremonial candles in lacquered holders are placed. New. $30-50

Purple and orange ceremonial robes with the tiny neck openings indicating their use by children. When they become thirteen years of age, they go with their families to a Shinto temple for a blessing.

A lower body garment worn with the robe above.

Sheer black ro silk priest's underkimono. This one has a label in the neck. Late Showa period. $150-250

Sheer brown undergarment and kesa of sheer white material with supplementary weft-woven mountains and a glass circle to secure the garment. Tassels of dip-dyed purple and white. This type of weave is called *sha*. Early Taisho. *Private collection*.

A formal men's set of blue and white stencil printed cotton. It would have been worn by a middle class person during the Taisho period on ceremonial occasions. $300-350

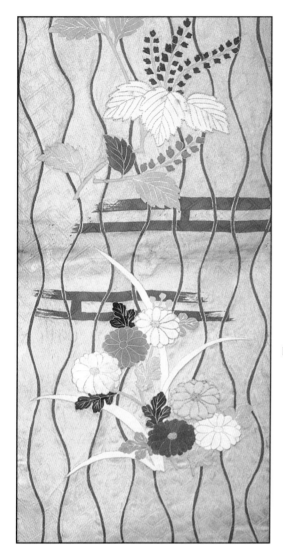

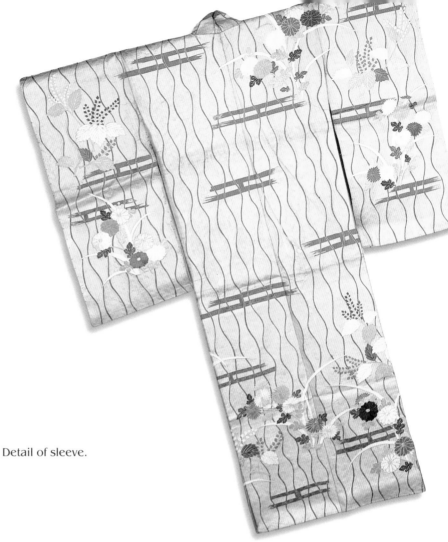

Detail of sleeve.

Fu Si - most likely a Noh costume called a *atsuita*, worn for a male's role. It is red paper and cotton combined with surihaku gold leaf all over. Flowers are either hand painted or embroidered with couched thread detailing. Late Meiji. $3000-4000

Detail of couching and embroidery.

14. Contemporary Wearable Art

Many creative people throughout the world today respect the fine textiles of Japan and find ways to include them in their wearable art works. A handful of talented sewers, both professional and non-professional, whose work gives new life to vintage textiles, represent the group.

Artists Represented

A Thousand Cranes- This company in New York uses scraps of vintage Japanese fabric to create a variety of items. They are business-to-business only.

Connie Chew- From New York, she numbers and signs each scarf Onomik (kimono spelled backward). She considers the combination of parts an art in itself, and exhibits her unique expression with the Japanese textiles she uses.

June Colburn- Her career as a noted international designer reflects years living abroad. She is a sought after national teacher and lecturer on Oriental design. She says, "the artists and craftsmen who created stylish, elegant kimono studied for decades to master their art. It seems important to honor both the artistry of the kimono and the memory of their former owners by designing quilts and clothing which will share this rich legacy." June Colburn Designs incorporate vintage Japanese material. She resides in Florida.

Lois Ericson- Her company, Design and Sew Patterns, has several styles that utilize vintage kimono. She is a self taught designer, author, sewing enthusiast and artist. She has written over fourteen books, and numerous articles for sewing magazines. Because of her affinity to Oriental culture, she thinks perhaps, though Swedish, she was Japanese in a former life. Lois lives in Oregon.

Stephanie Kimura- From Hawaii, she is of Japanese descent. She incorporates Japanese aesthetic into pattern she designed that is crazy quilted and dimensional using vintage kimono.

Katherine Koumoutseas was born in Greece and lives near Washington, D.C. Recipient of the International Women in Design Award for textiles in 1984 and the Annie Albers Bauhaus Award from Renwick Gallery in 1986, she designed for Arise in the 1990s.

Carol Lane-Saber- Living in Washington state, she is a fiber artist and teacher, specializing in the use of Japanese textiles. Carol has won awards for her work, and leads tours to Japan to educate and inspire people, and to collect more kimono and other related items.

Masako Ogura- She grew up in Japan in a house her mother, a dancer, filled with traditional music, art and culture. She was taught the appreciation and subtleties of wearing kimono. Masako now lives in New York City and is a costume designer for theater and television. She tries to honor the original kimono artist's vision in her handbag creations.

Gladys Riddell- A retired medical school teacher from South Africa, now living in the United States. She has sewn and beaded for many years, occasionally taking classes and incorporating techniques learned into her own designs. She enjoys the feel and challenge of working with different silks.

Carol Schneider- An editor at a large publishing house, she also makes vests, scarves and other new items from old kimono and other fabric. She resides in New York.

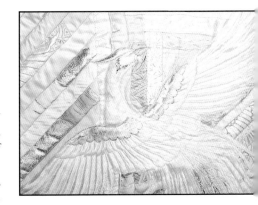

Detail of piecing and quilting from a wall hanging by June Colburn

"Keiko" - Wall quilt by June Colburn using vintage Japanese fabrics.

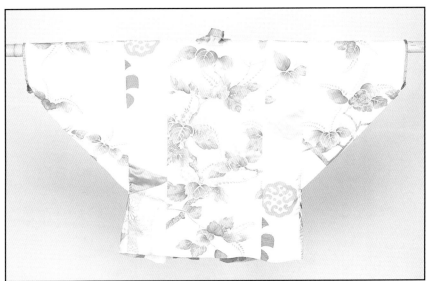

Back of a jacket by Gladys Riddell

Spring green and peach colors of vintage fabrics are used by Carol Schneider in her tunic. Her vest uses a bold magenta patterned kimono fabric.

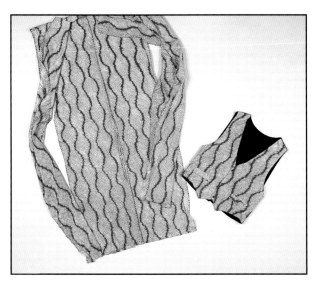

The vest front was made from the sleeves of a kimono, and what remains is shown next to it - enough to make a few more, or something else. The technique is shibori.

Cummerbunds and bow ties made from vintage kimono material. *Kathy Koumoutseas for Arise*

Group of hand-sewn purses made from vintage kimono by Masako Ogura. She grew up in Japan where her mother, a professional dancer, maintained a traditional household and taught her to appreciate the artistry of kimono. Masako is now a costume designer living in New York City.

Fragrant soaps are wrapped in kimono silk and tied with cords secured with Chinese coins. *A Thousand Cranes, New York City.*

Silk sachets with ties and eye pillows made from vintage material. *A Thousand Cranes, New York City.*

Selection of blank cards incorporating vintage fabric and handmade paper. *A Thousand Cranes, New York City.*

Pieces of vintage kimono are combined to an elegant effect by Onomik. The artist combines similar colors, and the details in the fabrics invite closer examination.

Reverse side of Onomik scarves.

Pair of scarves by Onomik using larger pieces. Black scarf incorporates shibori from a man's *heko obi*.

A Thousand Cranes takes a color block approach to the piecing of vintage kimono.

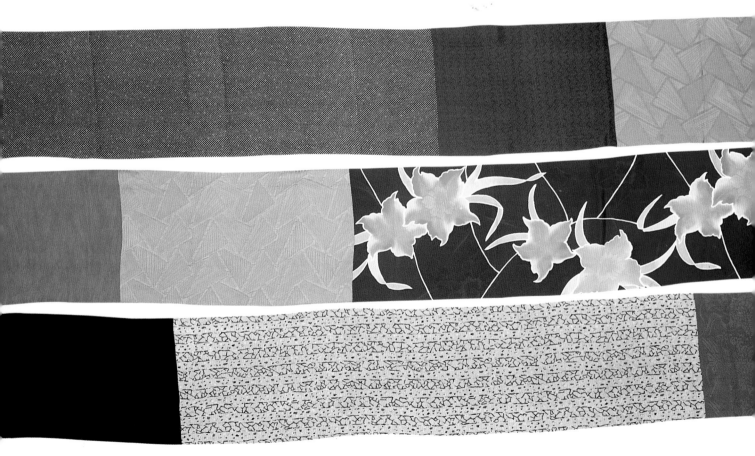

Reverse side of scarves.

June Colburn appliques flowers she has cut from damaged or soiled kimono and gives them new life on a jeans jacket. Front view. *Photo courtesy of designer.*

Back view of jacket

A simple adaptation of the basic kimono form into a women's three-quarter length jacket by Kathy Koumoutseas for Arise.

Group of four women's V-neck blouses with covered buttons. Each incorporates two to three vintage kimono into the design. *The Go Collection by Arise.*

Camp shirts made from vintage kimono fabric with covered buttons. *The Go Collection by Arise.*

Vest of kimono material in rust by Kathy Koumoutseas for Arise, and fan vest by June Colburn with crane design, made of pieces of various kimono and obi fabric from her pattern.

Designer Carol Schneider uses a bold magenta patterned kimono fabric and Chinese frog closures on the tunic, and two different gray fabrics for the vest. A neck scarf is whimsically wound around the head for an instant hat.

Stripes are not often thought of as being a Japanese motif, but they occur frequently, perhaps in unusual combinations of colors. Here, the back of a tunic vest and scarf by Carol Schneider show a variety of vintage kimono fabrics.

Vests in vintage Japanese fabric by Kathy Koumoutseas for Arise. The middle one is reversible, and the one with lapels is designed for formal use with a tuxedo shirt.

Two wearable artists are represented here. The tunic vest is made with ikat fabric, and the scarf from a combination of materials by Carol Schneider. The blouse is made from marbleized kimono silk and a lightweight wool by Lois Ericson from a pattern of her own design.

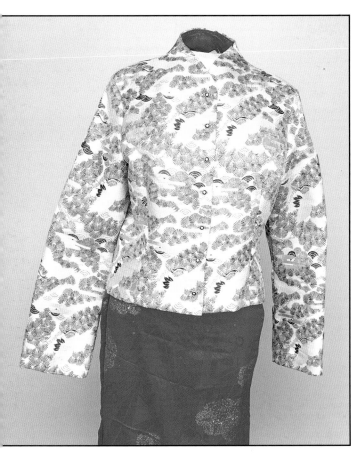

Short fitted jacket made of
obi material lined in fiery red
nagajuban fabric. Designed
by Gladys Riddell.

Over six different vintage fabrics were
artfully combined into this vest,
which has a unique open back design
by Stephanie Kimura.

"Flash" crazy pieced vest using
different red vintage fabrics,
including shibori, by Kimura.

Fan vest done in shades of red and turquoise
by June Colburn from her pattern.

Pieced kimono jacket made from a bundle of various textiles - obi,
kimono, and haori, accented with delicate bead work by Gladys Riddell.

Fiber artist June Colburn combines tiny figures with mini-kimono on this wall hanging called "Kimono Too." Its parts consist of small pieces of vintage kimono with a background and border of blue material.

Detail of wall quilt.

White on white with accents of silver, made from a vintage wedding kimono by piecing and then quilted by June Colburn.

"Fine Feathers Make a Fine Bird" wall quilt by June Colburn, from her pattern, made from vintage fabric. *Photo courtesy of designer*

Pillows by June Colburn of kimono and obi fabrics. The cat is called *Maneki Neko*, the welcoming cat, as seen in many Japanese homes and businesses in ceramic form. *Photo courtesy of designer*

Detail of "Tomesode Fan" wall quilt by June Colburn. The yuzen design of the hem of this garment lends itself so well to an adaptation like this when the garment is damaged, or you want to be more creative in the way to display and preserve the textile. The cord of the fan is dimensional, projecting slightly out from the surface.

"Fantasy Tokyo Dinner Party" was made in
1991 by Carol Lane Saber and won a prize in
the Fairfield Fashion Show, a nationwide
wearable art competition. It was made from
a pattern of her own design and incorporates
wedding kimono embroidery inserts. The
blouse and pants have insets of shibori.
*Photo courtesy of The Fairfield Processing
Company.*

This evening outfit from Carol Lane Saber has pieces of kimono patchworked into the jacket. *Photo by David Lee Bayliss.*

Detail of patchwork. *Photo by David Lee Bayliss.*

Opposite page:
"Blue Fandango" is made of Thai silk with appliques of silk from a young girl's kimono that have been embellished. Some of the kimono "flowers" are free standing, anchored to the garment only at the centers. *Designed and sewn by Carol Lane Saber. Photo by L.A. Clever*

Bibliography

Gluckman, Dale Carolyn and Sharon Sadako Takeda. *When Art Became Fashion: Kosode in Edo Period Japan*. New York: Weatherhill, Inc. for the Los Angeles Museum of Art . 1992.

Kawakatsu, Kenichi. "*Kimono*." Tokyo: Japan Travel Bureau. 1936.

Kennedy, Alan. *Japanese Costume, History and Tradition*. Paris: Konecky & Konecky. 1980.

Stevens, Rebecca and Yoshiko Wada, ed. *The Kimono Inspiration: Art and Art to Wear in America*. San Francisco: Pomegranate Artbooks for The Textile Museum, Washington, D.C. 1996.

Yamanaka, Norio. *The Book of Kimono*. New York: Kodansha International Ltd. 1982

Wada, Yoshiko, Mary Kellogg Rice, and Jane Barton. *Shibori: The Inventive Art of Japanese Shaped Resist Dyeing*. New York: Kodansha International/USA Ltd. 1983.

Glossary

bokashi - a technique of dip dyeing the inside hem of a woman's kimono, popular in the 1970s. A white lining begins to change color about 5 inches above the hem. Usually rust tones, a blush of color begins, moving into a vivid tone.

chirimen - thick crepe silk

chokochokogi - an informal reference to informal kimono used "to go here and there."

chuburisode - a kimono having a sleeve length nearly a yard long

chuya obi - an obi having two distinct sides, for greater versatility.

date eri - a collar cover for a kimono

do chu gi - a hip length large outer jacket for women, with attached overlapping ties. Often meisen ikat.

fudangi - a kimono worn to go to work, or for running errands, but not for visiting.

fukuro obi - usually decorated on one side only, this is used for semi formal and formal dress.

fukusa - a formal square shaped cloth used in the presentation or display of gifts

furisode - a young, single woman's kimono, with long sleeves. Worn for coming of age ceremonies, and other formal occasions.

furoshiki - this can be lowly cotton reinforced with thick stitches at the corners or high grade silk, hand painted. It is a square cloth to wrap or carry things.

genrokusode - a short rounded sleeve found on a married woman's or a working woman's kimono

go sho dolls - originally a memento of visits to the royal court, these dolls represent boys about 5 years old. They are charming images that are usually found on children's and men's kimono.

getta - wood sandals with two vertical parallel pieces about two inches high, worn with informal kimono or yukata

hakama -worn by men and occasionally women, a divided, pleated skirt.

haori - a short silk jacket worn by both men and women over the longer kimono

heko obi - man's long soft silk obi, usually having shibori tie dye designs at either end used to secure the nagajuban or worn at home in informal circumstances.

homongi - a woman's kimono worn for going out on visiting occasions.

ita jime - a form of dyeing using boards to tightly clamp fabric to resist dyes

jun hitoe -a single layer kimono worn in summertime

juban - a kimono shaped under garment

kakeshita or *shiromuku* kimono - both are names for the kimono worn under the uchikake during a wedding ceremony.

kaku obi - a narrow stiff obi, usually worn to secure men's kimono.

kamishimo - the top part of a formal men's costume, having wing-like shoulders, of supported, stiffened material

kasuri - splashed cloth, or ikat . A process whereby either or both the weft and the warp are bound and dyed, being unbound and re-bound for as many colors as were in the design, before being woven. This painstaking process results in the pattern apppearing on the loom as it is woven. Meisen ikat became a standard as women entered the work force in the early part of the century, as it did not easily wrinkle or show soil. Cotton kasuri made with indigo dyes was seen frequently on farms.

katazome - a stenciled design, most often produced in Japanese textiles by using rice paste resist, although sometimes wax is used, much like batiked cloth.

kesa - a priest's garment, sometimes made from scrap material.

kimono - a long robe of silk worn by men and women, that has evolved with few changes since the seventh century in Japan

kosode - prior to the Edo era, this was what we refer to as kimono, but actually means a sleeve opening which is small. Also a way to classify sleeve length,from longest to shortest.

kumihimo - ties that are woven in many distinctive patterns from thin silk cords, or infrequently, strung beads, used as closures on women's haori. Men's haori used a thicker, longer cord, often white, though sometimes of a thin flat weave.

jun-hitoe - single layered kimono, worn in summertime.

meisen ikat - a woven fabric that has had both warp and weft threads resisted and dyed prior to the final set up of the loom and weaving, so as to produce a preplanned design. Can also be produced by stencils cut to look like ikat edges or machine printed.

michiyuki - a double breasted overcoat, worn by women to protect kimono

mon - a family crest

nagagi - type of kimono that is medium formal for special occasions and visiting.

nagajuban - undergarment, shaped like a kimono with fully open sleeves, usually made of silk

Nagoya obi - designed in the early part of the twentieth century to be lighter and easier to wear than the double fold obi, it has about three feet of fourteen-inch-wide material, with the rest of the length folded in half.

nui - the general term for embroidery.

obi - the wide silk sash that secures the kimono and ties in the back in a variety of ways. Usually 12 to 14 feet in length, there are many different types classified by how it is woven, where it is from, its formality or use for casual wear.

obi age - soft silk sashes used to secure kimono. Often they have dimensional shibori. Edges of obi age peak out at the top of the obi, like a fancy trim.

obi jime - cords about 3 feet in length that are tied around the wide obi to help secure the obi bow.

oburisode - the sleeves of a furisode that are the longest

okashizome - combination of a hand painted and a dip dyed technique of textile design

Oshima - a particularly valued type of ikat woven textile, usually in tones of brown from mordants used to set the dyes.

rinzu - a type of figured silk that is compared to jacquard

ro - a type of sheer weave that resembles horizontal rows

sakiori obi - a country style obi, yet often elegantly woven in interesting patterns from strips of discarded kimono.

sha - a type of sheer weave that is lightweight for summer use.

shibori - a simple way of describing it would be tie dye. By using cotton or silk cloth that is already woven, different methods of sectioning off areas and applying dye to others has been developed into many complex and fascinating patterns over centuries by the Japanese.

shi chi go san - in November, children of 7 (shi chi) 5 (go) and 3 (san) are brought to the temples for blessing ceremonies. This term of most often applied to the boy's kimono.

sumi-e - here used to describe the designs in black ink that are drawn free hand upon silk for decoration.

surihaku - gold leaf or gold painted accents on cloth.

tabi - cotton or nylon ankle length socks designed to be worn with sandals.

tatouchi - rice paper used to wrap kimono for storage.

tomesode - usually black with a yuzen decorated hem, this is the most formal woman's kimono, worn by the wedding party members, or other formal occasions.

tsuke obi - a pre-tied obi, easily clipped on in two pieces

tsukesage - Kimono design that covers the back from shoulder to hem and is also repeated with variation on the left lower front and right sleeve. Mostly on nagagi, dressy visiting kimono.

tsumugi - a handwoven silk made from leftover cocoons. Highly prized by the Japanese.

uchikake - the very long kimono worn without an obi that is customarily a part of the bride's outfit. Its origins were in the Muromachi (1338-1568) period.

yukata - a cotton robe worn in summer, for dancing, or after the bath.

yuzen - the art of painting on silk with a resisted area was introduced by a man from Kyoto during the Genroku period (1688-1704), Miyazaki Yuzensai. He used rice paste mixed with soybeans and salt, that was stored in a container like a pastry bag, and the tip used to make a design that was more free than the traditional stencils.

zome - a general term to describe stencil process to dye cloth

zori - fancy sandals worn by women often in material to match their kimono

Index